The Parents' Resource Book

by Gail Granet Velez

Illustrations by Pat Tobin

A PLUME BOOK

NEW AMERICAN LIBRARY

NEW YORK AND SCARBOROUGH, ONTARIO

Note to the Reader

The ideas, procedures, and suggestions contained in this book are
not intended as a substitute for consulting with your physician. All
matters regarding your health require medical supervision.

PLUME TRADEMARK REG. U.S. PAT. OFF. AND FOREIGN COUNTRIES
REGISTERED TRADEMARK—MARCA REGISTRADA
HECHO EN HARRISONBURG, VA., U.S.A.

SIGNET, SIGNET CLASSIC, MENTOR, PLUME, MERIDIAN and
NAL BOOKS are published *in the United States* by New American Library,
1633 Broadway, New York, New York 10019, *in Canada* by The New
American Library of Canada Limited, 81 Mack Avenue, Scarborough,
Ontario M1L 1M8

Library of Congress Cataloging-in-Publication Data

Granet Velez, Gail.
  The parents' resource book.

  Includes index.
  1. Parenting—United States. 2. Child rearing—United States. I. Title.
HQ755.8.G72   1986   649'.1   85-31989
ISBN 0-452-25739-5

First Printing, May, 1986

1 2 3 4 5 6 7 8 9

PRINTED IN THE UNITED STATES OF AMERICA

TO THE MILLIONS OF PARENTS WHO WANT TO MAKE THEIR LIVES LESS HECTIC AND MORE REWARDING...

Gail Granet Velez has dedicated these terrific time- and money-saving ideas to all those parents, to make their lives less hectic and more rewarding and enjoyable. Aside from the thousands of where-to-go, who-to-ask, and how-to guidelines, she's included lots of practical facts, such as how to get chewing gum out of a child's hair, sizing charts for clothes, and when to choose between buying sneakers and shoes. And, step-by-step, she takes parents through all the major and minor decisions they're likely to face—in the best, most up-to-date resource guide for parents of newborns to five-year-olds.

THE PARENTS' RESOURCE BOOK

GAIL GRANET VELEZ is the mother of two and the editor of *The Little People's Directory.* She is also the publisher of the Parents' Press *Family Entertainment Guide,* the ultimate answer to what to do with children in the New York metropolitan area.

To my loveable & high-spirited sons

Acknowledgments

I am deeply indebted to the following people who supported me, gave of their time and expertise, and offered their good counsel. Janet Gilmartin Ono, Emily DiMartino, Liz Mayers, Donna Margolis, Janet Papolas, Joel Fram, Al and Carla Weintraub, Mark Wein, Seymour Teicher, Said Saber, Josh Kronen, Stephanie Farrow, Janet Kleinman, Howard Kaufman, M.D., Vicki Semel, Ph.D., Roger Granet, M.D., Valerie Granet, Edward J. Piesman, D.M.D., William Semel, M.D., Elisabeth Bing, Lona Tannenbaum, Ed.D., Irwin Gedinsky, Barry Krumholtz, Pam Scurry, Sonny Oshon, Lynn Janson-Guyer, Joanne Boeckelman Pre-School Association of Child Care, Inc., Jean Schultz, Mark Levine, Patricia Dooley, Cathleen Sabo, Lynn Weisman, Barbara Opotowsky, Ozzie Schwartz, Don Leftt, Patricia Tobin, Pat Berrins, Pamela McDougal, Shelia Morreno, Roberta Columbus, Carol Greilsheimer, Celia Woodley, The American Camping Association, and The United States Consumer Product Safety Commission.

And finally, a very special thanks to my patient and perceptive editor, Carole Hall, my parents, and Dr. Sergio Rothstein.

Contents

9. Favorite Toys, Arts and Crafts, and Pets 144

10. Books, Magazines, and Music for Children 164

11. Playing and Learning with Other Kids 185

Appendix A. Memories 206

Appendix B. Resources for Parents 208

Appendix C. Your Household Employee and Social Security 210

Appendix D. Mail Order 213

Appendix E. Reading for Parents 216

Index 221

Introduction

Recently, after dropping off my 9-year-old son Erik and my 6-year-old son Marc at school, I decided to treat myself to a cup of coffee and a homemade scone at Zabar's before rushing off to work. It wasn't work that was preoccupying me but rather the 25 6-year-olds who were invited to Marc's birthday party on Saturday. As I sipped my coffee, I thought about that sunny December day with freshly falling snow when we brought Erik home from the hospital. Everything was ready for him. His room was vibrant with colors of red, yellow, and blue and the figures of Raggedy Ann and Andy were waiting to greet him. As I gently took off the bunting and sweater and hat set, I felt like I was unwrapping a very precious gift. I had an overwhelming feeling of love and awe.

Three-and-a-half-years later on a lovely day in June with sounds and smells of summer in the air, Erik welcomed home his new brother Marc by waving a bouquet of balloons. Our loveable Irish setter, Autumn, licked Marc's little face in greeting. All of us shared the same mixture of love and awe towards this very special bundle. As I reminisced, Marc's birthday party seemed more and more like a celebration and less and less like a chore.

My children are on their way. No more babies at home. I have survived six strollers, 1,000 hours of shopping for clothes, toys, books, 4,000 diapers, 400 gallons of apple juice, tons of dirty laundry, ear aches, high fevers, the fussy-eating stage, toilet training, three gerbils, four goldfish and one snake, the uncertainty of selecting pediatricians, dentists, baby-sitters, schools, activities, camps, organizing 14 birthday parties, playdates, playgroups........and so will you!

Basic Decisions of Parenting

The Parents' Resource Book deals with the basic tasks and decisions that you will be faced with as parents. The guide will provide you with relevant facts and information on key topics to help you make sound selections and decisions. Some decisions will be of major importance (selecting a pediatrician, a nursery school, a day-care center, a camp, or a full-time housekeeper); other choices, while less significant, will definitely enhance the quality of your child's life (books, bedroom furniture and accessories, records, toys, birthday parties, the right family pet, etc.). While the loving and sharing is the most enjoyable part of parenting, the everyday tasks, decisions, and selections that parents make take a great deal of time, energy, and money. When these practical decisions of parenting are not planned for properly, or decisions are made without relevant facts, the results will be a drain on your energy and budget, and give you less quality time for loving and enjoying your children.

How to Use The Parents' Resource Book

The information in this book is designed in a directory format to make all kinds of information accessible to you when you need it. No wading through pages and pages to find the main concept of key facts on a specific topic. This guide is to be used as an on-going reference resource to meet the needs of your growing child. It's time to select the layette, crib, and carriage for your expected baby, turn to pages 33–34, 47–50, 65–69. What do you want in a pediatrician, turn to pages 77–78. It's time to child-proof the house, turn to pages 99–100. Oh no, chocolate ice-cream all over Jennie's new party dress, turn to page 60. Ready to plan that first birthday party, turn to page pages 202–203. How to find and evaluate toddler programs, turn to page 189. Whoops, the fussy-eating stage, turn to page 12, etc.

Each chapter gives you an overview of everything you need to know—the facts, options for different age groups and life-styles, and safety considerations—as well as how to evaluate quality products and services. *The Parents' Resource Book* will increase the pleasures and decrease the frustrations of living with and loving "Little People."

Wishing you a healthy and joyful
first five years.

Gail Granet Velez

CHAPTER 1

Good Food, Happy Meals

Feeding your newborn is the beginning of a rich family experience, where parent and child learn about each other. From the first suckle through later years (including the ones when all you hear is "Pass this," or "I don't want that") mealtime remains a special time, when the family reunites to laugh, share, and be together. Naturally, how you start to feed your baby depends on many practical and philosophical issues, and the choice is entirely up to you. Here's a survey of your options.

Breast-Feeding

You will need relatively few supplies:

- Nursing pads and shields
- Nursing bras
- Nightgowns and nursing tops
- Breast pump (optional)

If you are thinking about breast-feeding, you should begin to obtain information on it by the beginning of your last trimester of pregnancy. Studies have shown that babies receive immunity to a variety of infections through the mother's colostrum and milk, and that breast-feeding saves time and money. Speak with your obstetrician, midwife, or other mothers that have breast-fed. Contact the La Leche League, a national breast-feeding information and support organization for parents. The League has a series of helpful discussion groups as well as

1

valuable publications. To locate a League Leader in your area, call or write the national headquarters:

La Leche League International
9616 Minneapolis Avenue
P.O. Box 1209
Franklin Park, IL 60131-8209

(312) 455-7730
(312) 451-1819 Mail order department for publications and free catalog

If you are a working mother, it would be especially helpful to make contact with this group for suggestions on balancing work and breast-feeding. See Appendix for bibliography of reading material on Breast-feeding.

Bottle Feeding

Those of us who prefer, choose, or decide to supplement breast-feeding with bottle feeding, will become experts on formulas, usually a combination of cow's milk, water, sugar, and other nutrients such as iron. Ask your obstetrician or pediatrician for advice and recommendations on homemade or prepared formulas.

Prepared Formulas

Prepared formulas come in cans or bottles already sterilized. There are two types. The *ready-to-use* formula can be poured directly into sterilized bottles or the disposable plastic nursing bags. The *concentrated prepared* formula must be diluted with water. You can mix the concentrated formula with sterilized water and pour into sterilized bottles or disposable plastic nursing bags or dilute with tap water and sterilize the bottles and formula together (see page 5).

Choosing a Bottle

Standard bottles come in a variety of materials. Clear, rigid plastic bottles are stain resistant, unbreakable, and easy to clean. It's best to avoid using opaque flexible plastic bottles, because they hold stains and absorb odors. It is also difficult to see how much liquid is in such bottles. Sometimes they are shaped like cartoon characters. Baby may enjoy the novelty, but I wouldn't recommend everyday use. Glass bottles are easier to clean, but because they are breakable, they can't be used when the baby begins to hold the bottle.

You'll need eight bottles (four 8-oz. bottles, four 4-oz. bottles). Each bottle will need a set of nipples, caps and rings, plus three to six spare nipples and caps.

Bottle Supplies

You'll also need the following supplies:

- Bottle brush
- Nipple brush
- Tongs
- Sterilizer or large covered pot with bottle rack (optional, depending on the advice of your pediatrician. If you use disposable plastic nursing bags, you won't need it at all).
- Can and jar opener
- Jars with tops, for storing sterilized items (nipples, pacifiers, caps and rings for bottles). Jars should be made of material that is easy to sterilize.
- A box of toothpicks
- Car bottle warmer to plug into the car's cigarette lighter. Great for traveling (optional).
- Insulated pouches for traveling or when you are on the go with baby. Can keep baby's bottle cold or warm.

Cleaning the Bottles

It is easier if you wash bottles, nipples, caps, and rings soon after they are used. Wash equipment with bottle and nipple brush in a mild soap and water solution. You can twist a toothpick through the nipple hole to clear the passageway. After you clean, stand bottles upside down to drain.

Sterilizing Feeding Equipment

Check with your pediatrician about sterilizing your feeding equipment. Some feel it is important, whereas others believe that washing bottles and accessories in a dishwasher is acceptable.

If you decide sterilizing is important, you can use a large covered pot with a bottle rack or buy a stovetop sterilizer or an electric sterilizer. The sterilizers usually come with rack, bottles, caps, and tongs. Some electric models have an automatic cutoff mechanism to prevent accidental overheating, which can occur when the sterilizer is not turned off at the scheduled time. This can be an important feature because many times parents get preoccupied with other tasks with the newborn and can easily forget about the sterilizers. (I burned a sterilizer because I was busy comforting my son who had just awakened. The smell of burned plastic remained in my house for 48 hours.) If you don't want an electric model, set an alarm clock to remind you to turn off the sterilizer.

Sterilizing Methods

Terminal method. Put formula made with unsterilized water into unsterilized bottles and then sterilize them all together in a sterilizer or large covered pot. For detailed information on this method check Dr. Benjamin Spock's *Baby and Child Care* (Pocket Books, 1981).

Aseptic method. The most convenient method of preparing bottles in the most moderate price range is to sterilize the equipment by itself and then put sterile formula into bottles. Here's how to do it: In the sterilizer or large pot place bottles upside down in the rack. Then place nipples, rings, caps, or any other equipment that needs to be sterilized such as a can opener or pacifiers in the sterilizer. Put several inches of water in the bottom of the pot or sterilizers, cover, and follow the manufacturer's direction for heating and cooling time. If you are using a pot, bring water to a boil and then let it boil rapidly for 5 more minutes. Then let cool. After the bottles cool, pour ready-to-use formula into bottles, and screw on nipples in the rings. Cover with caps. Refrigerate until ready to use. To take the chill out of the bottle, soak in hot water. To test the temperature of the liquid, squirt a drop on your wrist.

Easier Options

Disposable plastic nursing bags fitted into a plastic frame. The formula is then poured directly into the bag. When empty, the bag is disposed of. Although these disposable bags save time because you don't have to scrub or sterilize the frame, you still have to sterilize the nipples, rings, and caps that fit over it; sometimes the bags leak. It is also difficult to measure how much the baby drinks.

Disposable bottles filled with ready-to-use formula. These bottles come in six-packs. They need no refrigeration. Because they are the most expensive option, it is not practical to use them on an ongoing basis, but they're great for the first day home from the hospital, for traveling, or for the breast-fed baby who needs an occasional bottle. Make sure these bottles have disposable nipples attached with a cap too, for total convenience.

Tips on Nipples

- Newborn babies like smaller nipples, whereas older babies seem to prefer the longer ones.
- If a nipple hole is too small, it can frustrate a baby.
- To enlarge a hole of a nipple, first boil the nipple, then insert a toothpick while it is cooling.
- Boiling a nipple can reduce the size of the nipple hole.
- Discard nipples that become too soft or when the hole is too big.

Bottle-Feeding Safety Tips

- Babies should always be held and supervised while being fed a bottle; resist the temptation to use mechanical bottle proppers.
- During feeding, make sure that the milk is filling the nipple and top of the bottle so that baby is not sucking in air along with the milk.
- Severe tooth decay can be caused by allowing a baby to drift slowly off to sleep while sucking a bottle of milk or juice. The American Dental Association recommends giving babies only water in the bedtime bottle and never putting sugar in the water so baby will drink it in a bottle. (See page 83 on Dental Care.)
- Never let baby hold a glass bottle by himself.

How to Burp Your Baby

- Always put a cloth diaper on you to catch any spit ups.
- Hold baby against your shoulder. Gently pat or stroke the back in a semicircle in between the shoulder blades.
- Lay baby on your lap stomach down, with his head turned to the side and pat gently or stroke.
- Have baby sit up on your lap tilted forward; gently hold baby's chin with your thumb and index finger. Allow baby to lean against your arm.

• You can burp your baby in the middle of a feeding and at the end.

Pacifier Safety

Many babies need extra sucking experience that pacifiers provide. The U.S. Consumer Product Safety Commission requires all pacifiers manufactured in the United States to:

• Have two ventilation holes in shields to allow air passage.
• Have following warning label: "Warning: Do not tie pacifier around child's neck because it presents a strangulation danger."
• Pass a "pull test" after boiling and cooling to assure that they will not come apart.
• Be sure that the protrusions on the backs of shields are regulated in size to prevent ingestion.
• Be sure the pacifiers you use conform to those standards.

Baby's First Solids

I will always remember the puzzled look on my son's face the first time he tasted cottage cheese, and his look of sheer delight at his first taste of chocolate cake. I remember, too, the day I raced all over my neighborhood looking for a ripe banana with just the right number of brown spots, because the pediatrician told me to introduce bananas on Tuesday!

Your pediatrician will tell you when it is time to introduce your baby to solid foods. When that time comes, you'll need a seat with a restraining system, some special equipment, and a few clever ideas more than you'll need a perfect banana!

Your Baby's High Chair

Before your baby can sit up, you can use an infant seat during feedings. Once your baby can sit firmly by himself (around 6 months), you can begin to use a high chair. Until your baby is 2 years old, he needs a high chair while he is eating. With a high chair, your baby can be near you while you're working in the kitchen, have a safe and convenient place for arts and craft projects, and be near you when you are having your dinner. (Sometimes that works!) If you eat out a lot or visit friends with your 6- to 24-month-old, consider getting a portable high chair.

Children 2 years and older who can balance on your dining room chairs but need a little bit more height to reach the top of the table comfortably appreciate booster seats. Here are some buying guidelines for each of these options.

What to Look For in a High Chair

- Can the chair be cleaned? Chrome and vinyl are easier to clean than wood.
- Can the tray be cleaned easily? Is the tray detachable? Will the tray fit in your kitchen sink?
- Trays that extend back under the arms catch spills.
- Can the tray be moved to various positions (nearer or farther from the child) to accommodate the growing child?
- If possible, bring your baby to the store to try out the high chair. I bought a high chair without my son. It seemed easy to manage in the store, but when I tried to lift my son in and out, I needed a third hand—two hands to move the tray and one hand to hold and lift the baby.
- A larger tray will provide more space for mealtime, playing, or doing an art project.
- The surface of the tray should be level. My first high chair had slanted arms and everything slid toward my son, landing on his lap.
- The high chair legs should have a wide stance for stability.
- Look for sharp edges and openings that might injure a baby's hands or fingers.
- See that there is a space between the chair back and the seat so that you can easily sponge off caked-in food.
- Look for an adjustable footrest.

The Portable High Chair

Use from 6 months to 2 to 3 years. Begin to use when baby is sitting up firmly. Stop using when the child can balance on your dining room chairs without the need for a restraining system. You can travel with the seat to use at restaurants and at homes of relatives and friends. It is lightweight and self-adjusts to fit almost any table or counter. However, it should not be used on glass-topped tables. The baby should not be left unsupervised in these portable high chairs.

High Chair Safety

- Check safety features. Secure locking devices will prevent chair from collapsing with children in them.
- The tray should lock firmly into place.
- A sturdy restraining system should include waist and crotch belts. If you are not satisfied with high-chair restraining system, you can use a shoulder harness and attach straps to the high chair.
- Always use restraining system.
- Always double-check to be sure that the tray is properly locked in place.
- Never leave baby unattended in the high chair.
- See that your baby can't reach anything dangerous (appliances, cords, tablecloths, etc.).

Booster Seat

Use from 2 years and up. Begin to use when your child can balance on your dining room chairs without the need for a restraining system but needs a little height to reach the top of the table comfortably. They are portable, so they can be used at restaurants or at homes of friends or relatives as needed.

More Helpful Equipment

Small Vegetable Steamer

The vegetable steamer is a good way to cook fruits and vegetables for the entire family. The steamer uses only a little water, so valuable vitamins are not destroyed. The fruits and vegetables sit on a rack placed in the pot. Cover and cook for the recommended time. Steamers are also for warming up food.

Bibs

A bib will protect clothing from stains. For the young baby use small terry cloth bibs that tie at the neck to absorb spit up. As baby begins eating solid foods, use larger bibs that snap at the neck and reach to the knees. Remember, plastic is easy to clean!

Baby Food Grinders

Small pieces of food—fruit, vegetables, cooked chicken, and such can easily be ground into baby food. All you need is a small, manual grinder. It's easy to use and easy to clean.

Cleaning Up

As your children begin to show an interest in feeding themselves, you'll be amazed at the mess they can create and how far a spoonful of mashed peas can be flung across a room! The floor around the high chair can get particularly messy. A heavy piece of vinyl (4 × 4 feet) under the high chair will come in handy during every meal. If the high chair is placed near a wall, you can put transparent Con-tact paper on the wall for protection.

Food Preparation

The following tips on food preparation from *Baby Sense* by Frances Wells Burck (St. Martin, 1979) help assure that the food that your baby actually eats is good and nutritious.

Fruits and Vegetables
- Peel
- Cut up into small pieces
- Steam until soft
- Puree with baby grinder or food processor
- Buy ripe bananas with brown spots, mash with fork

For Thinning Food, Add Liquid
- Water
- Liquid from pot that vegetable or fruit was steamed in
- Milk
- Formula
- Breast milk
- Soup broth
- Juice

Thickening Food

- Wheat germ
- Whole grain cereal
- Arrowroot
- Cottage cheese
- Farmer cheese
- Cooked egg yolk
- Yogurt
- Mashed white or sweet potatoes

Serving Tips

- To warm food place in Pyrex dish in pan of water if you don't have an electric warmer.
- Canned food needs little heat.
- Baby food jars are not heat resistant. Remove food to warm.
- Some commercial baby food has all natural ingredients. Look at list of ingredients on label.
- Look at the safety button on the lid of baby food jar. If lid is concave, it means the jar is vacuum sealed.
- Don't feed baby from jar and reuse; the enzymes from saliva will spoil leftover food.
- Store opened jars in the refrigerator no more than 2 days.

Shopping for Food

- Avoid buying produce on Sundays or Monday mornings because stores usually do not receive shipments on Saturdays or Sundays.
- Do not wash produce until you are ready to use it. Washing often accelerates the molding process.
- Ripen fruit at room temperature and then refrigerate.
- Nutrition reminder—overcooking produce lessens the value of its vitamins, minerals, and roughage.
- Note expiration dates on packaged food products.

Healthy Snacks

You may want to check with your pediatrician or dentist before introducing these to your child.

- Pretzels (rub off excess salt)
- Dry cereal mix (e.g., Cheerios and raisins)
- Fresh fruits (cut fruit into thin slivers)
- Cheese

- Bagels
- Bagel chips
- Dry fruits
- Frozen yogurt, or yogurt and sprinkles

Feeding Your Older Child

Standby Meals for Fussy Eaters

Most children go through a fussy eating stage, and I learned the following facts from my kids as they were going through theirs.

- Pieces of things (onions, parsley, oregano, etc.) should not be seen on or in food. Puree or strain sauces or gravies.
- Food should be smooth and not lumpy.
- Serve small portions.
- Meat should be cut into small pieces with fat and veins removed.
- Children tend to generalize. If a child finds something wrong with one bite, he generalizes it to the remainder of the portion (sometimes this dislike can last for several weeks). If a child finds a vein or fat in a piece of meat, she might not only refuse to eat the rest of the portion because she feels it all has veins, but refuse that meat whenever it's served.
- Forget stews and casseroles. Combinations of food cooked together seem to turn off the fussy eater.
- Expect that any child who's visiting for lunch or dinner will have the "fussies," too.

Sure-to-Please Recipes

PENNY HAMBURGERS

Shape 1 pound of ground beef into quarter-sized hamburgers and cook as usual.
SERVINGS: 4 to 6

EASY HOMEMADE FRENCH FRIES

4 large baking potatoes
oil (fill half the pan)

salt (optional—sprinkle on after potatoes are removed from pan)

1. Peel the potatoes and cut into strips.
2. Heat oil in a frying pan on a high flame for 5 minutes, then reduce to a medium flame. Test the oil by putting one potato into the oil— if the potato turns golden brown, the oil is ready. If not, heat the oil a few minutes longer.
3. Slowly put the potatoes in the pan. The oil should cover the potatoes. Cook until the potatoes become golden brown. Remove from pan and drain on absorbent paper and cool for 5 minutes before serving.

SERVINGS: 4

MAKE-YOUR-OWN-TACOS

taco shells
shredded lettuce
cut-up tomatoes
American or cheddar cheese (shredded)
sliced cucumbers

small slices of avocado
rice
penny hamburgers (see page 12)
pieces of chicken

Put each ingredient on a small plate and let the children fix their own taco combination!

SERVINGS: 6 to 8

BITE-SIZE MEAT BALLS

1 pound chopped ground beef
salt
pepper
garlic powder

3 tablespoons olive oil
2 cups spaghetti sauce (see recipe on page 15)

1. Season meat lightly with salt, pepper, and garlic powder.
2. Make small balls.
3. Heat oil in large pan; brown the meat balls; drain off oil.
4. Place meat balls in spaghetti sauce and cook for 30 minutes.

SERVINGS: 4 to 6 (6 to 10 meat balls)

ONE-POT ROAST CHICKEN
AND POTATOES

2 whole chicken breasts   *paprika*
4 tablespoons oil   *celery*
salt   *dill*
pepper   *parsley*
garlic powder   *4 medium-sized baking potatoes*

1. Preheat oven to 375°.
2. Wash chicken, then place in roasting pan. Pour 2 tablespoons of oil on each. Then sprinkle salt, pepper, garlic powder, and paprika on both sides and rub into the chicken. Put celery, dill, and parsley inside each chicken breast.
3. Peel and cut potatoes into small pieces. Sprinkle remaining oil over the potatoes and dust with salt and paprika. Place around the chicken in the roasting pan. Cover with aluminum foil and bake for 2 hours.
4. Before serving, remove all skin and scrape off visible seasoning.
SERVINGS: 3 to 4

FRIED CHICKEN WITHOUT THE BONES

2 whole boneless chicken   *⅓ cup oil*
  breasts   *3 tablespoons butter or*
2 eggs   *margarine*
bread crumbs

1. Cut the chicken in half and cut away any excess fat. Pound the chicken by covering the pieces with wax paper and hitting chicken with heavy pan or mallet until thin.
2. Wash pieces, then dip in beaten eggs, then dip in bread crumbs.
3. Heat oil and butter (margarine) in a large skillet.
4. Cook the chicken cutlets until golden brown on each side.
SERVINGS: 2 to 3

CHICKEN SOUP a la CARTE

FOR SOUP STOCK

4 pounds chicken necks
2 whole chicken breasts
5 carrots (peeled)
2 onions
3 celery stalks
1 small parsnip
1 small turnip
1 bunch dill
1 bunch parsley
salt
pepper

TO SERVE WITH THE SOUP

4 carrots
1 package frozen small peas
8 oz box egg noodles

1. Wash first nine ingredients and add to 4 quarts of water.
2. Add salt and pepper.
3. Bring slowly to a boil. Then cover and simmer for 2 to 3 hours.
4. Drain and save the chicken breasts and stock. Drain fat from stock.
5. Save the white meat from the breasts and discard the bones.
6. In separate pots, steam carrots and cook peas and egg noodles. When serving, ask each child what they want in their soup. They have their choice of chicken, noodles, peas, and carrots.

SERVINGS: 4

SCRUMPTIOUS SPAGHETTI SAUCE

3 cups peeled, chopped plum
 tomatoes, fresh or canned (if
 canned, use the Italian kind)
3 tablespoons olive oil

2 or 3 cloves garlic (crushed)
½ teaspoon salt
pepper to taste
8 oz pasta

1. Boil tomatoes for 2 minutes. Cool, then peel, core, and cut into quarters.
2. Heat oil in large skillet and saute garlic about 3 minutes. Add tomatoes, salt, and pepper; mix well; puree or mash the tomatoes with a fork.
3. Bring mixture to boil, then reduce heat and simmer, uncovered, stirring occasionally for 60 minutes or until the sauce is thickened.
4. Serve hot over pasta.

SERVINGS: 4 to 6

You'll be home free the next day for lunch if you save the leftover sauce to spread over a bagel or thick slice of French bread and top with grated mozzarella and Parmesan cheese for a pizza.

VEGETABLE OR FRUIT BREADS OR MUFFINS

The following recipes are also favorites of mine. My kids love them and so do their nursery school friends. You can eat them for breakfast, as snacks, or with whipped cream or frosting for desserts. Let your children guess what is in the muffin. Some children may be reluctant to try a zucchini, pumpkin, or carrot muffin if they know what they're eating.

ZUCCHINI, CARROT, BANANA, OR SWEET POTATO MUFFINS

---

1 cup of either finely grated
   zucchini (unpeeled), mashed
   ripe bananas, cooked mashed
   sweet potatoes or carrots
¾ cup vegetable oil
1 cup sugar

2 eggs
1½ cups flour
1 tsp cinnamon
1 tsp baking powder
¾ tsp baking soda

1. Preheat oven to 350°.
2. Mix vegetable or fruit with oil, sugar, and eggs. Add the rest of the ingredients, and mix until batter is smooth.
3. Grease two 4½ × 8 inch loaf pans or 2 dozen muffin tins. Fill halfway with batter and bake until the center is springy or a toothpick stuck into the center comes out clean. Large loaves will take about 45 minutes to an hour to bake. Muffins should be done in about 15 minutes.

PUMPKIN BREAD OR MUFFINS

*1 cup pumpkin (canned or
  fresh)*
4 eggs
½ cup water
1 cup vegetable oil
1 cup molasses
1 cup dark brown sugar

*3 cups whole wheat or plain
  white flour*
1½ tsp salt
2 tsps baking soda
2 tsp cinnamon
1 tsp nutmeg
½ tsp cloves

1. Preheat oven to 350°.
2. If using fresh pumpkin, remove seeds, peel off the dark orange skin, and cut into 1-inch chunks. Cook over medium heat with a little water until tender, about 20 minutes. Drain and mash.
3. Mix pumpkin with eggs, water, oil, molasses, and brown sugar. Add the rest of the ingredients, and mix until the batter is smooth.
4. Grease two 4½ × 8 inch loaf pans or 2 dozen muffin tins. Fill halfway with batter and bake until the center is springy or a toothpick stuck into the center comes out clean. Large loaves will take about 45 minutes to an hour to bake. Small loaves will take about ½ hour, and muffins should be done in about 15 minutes.

YIELD: 24 muffins or 2 loaves

ALL-TIME FAVORITE SANDWICH FILLERS

Picky eaters may like these fillers without the bread, just served on a plate.

Peanut butter and jelly
Cream cheese
Grilled cheese
Plain tuna fish with mayonnaise

Hot dogs
Hamburgers
Bologna

Adventuresome eaters, of course, like variety as much as many grown ups. Try some of the quick, easy recipes in Jan Brink and Melinda Ramm's *S.N.A.C.K.S: Speedy, Nutritious and Cheap Kids' Snacks* (Plume/Signet, 1984) for fun.

Eating Out with Children

To get the most enjoyment when eating out with your children, call ahead and find out the following:

- Are there high chairs or booster seats? (Bring a harness or a belt to strap the child in.)
- Is there a children's menu?
- If it is not a family restaurant, ask what time you should come to get the fastest service.
- What is the usual waiting time to be served? If you think the wait will be too long for your child, pick another restaurant with faster service.
- Can you bring strollers, booster chair, or a portable high chair to the table?

After you are seated:

- Inform the waiter that you have a young child with you and would appreciate fast service.
- Ask the waiter to bring bread to the table as soon as possible.
- Do not order any food that will take an especially long time to prepare.
- Don't forget to move the water away from your child. It always spills.
- Sometimes it is helpful to have a small pad and pencil for children to doodle on. Bring a small soft toy for the very young child.

CHAPTER 2

Bathtime, Diaper, and Toilet-Training Tips

During the first couple of years, you'll spend a lot of time bathing your child and changing diapers. As your child becomes independent, you will be there to support her toilet-training efforts as well.

Bathtime

The following tips will help you organize this special time between you and your baby.

A Bathtub for Your Newborn Baby

Bathtubs for newborns are designed for use from the time your pediatrician tells you to start bathing your infant until he or she can sit up firmly unassisted (around 6 months). These tubs only hold a small amount of water so you can give your newborn a generous sponge bath with a minimum amount of splashing. Although an inexpensive plastic dishpan from any hardware or discount store will serve the same purpose, you may want to buy a tub especially designed for baby's bath. Before you make such a purchase, decide whether it is more comfortable for you to bathe the baby sitting in a chair, standing, kneeling, or sitting on the floor. Then choose a tub that will be comfortable for you to use. Some go in the sink, some in the bathtub, others on the floor or a table. Whichever style you choose, be sure it is sturdy and lightweight.

19

Organizing Bathtime Accessories and Supplies

You'll need to gather towels, washcloths, and the clothing that you will dress the baby in after the bath, *before* you get started. Hang baby's towel on a hook about 3 feet from the floor (at about 2 years of age, many children like to begin doing things for themselves, and at that time your child will be able to help himself to a towel if it's within easy reach).

Baby's Bathing Supplies

Keep the baby's toiletries together, including the soap. Store the soap in its own plastic case, separate from the family soap. Other supplies might include:

- Baby powder
- Baby shampoo
- Baby lotion
- Ointment for diaper rash
- Baby nail scissors
- Cotton swabs
- Diapers
- Masking tape (comes in handy when the tape on the disposable diapers does not stick)
- Premoistened towels
- Petroleum jelly

Shopping for Toiletries

You'll buy lots of toiletries for your baby during the first two years, so try to locate a store that discounts these items. Large toy discount stores often carry diapers and other infant supplies, as do many drugstores, department stores, and variety stores. If you have trouble finding a discount store, ask another mother!

Bath Toys

Bath toys make bathtime playtime for children of all ages. Your baby will enjoy watching a bath ball bob up and down. In time, he'll be reaching for it. Once your child begins to sit up without support in the tub, he can experience the water and toys as a wonderful avenue for play. To get maximum use out of bath toys, select items that can also be used out of water. Store the bath toys in a plastic net bag that you hang over your tub so the water can drain out of the bag.

Toy Suggestions

Brightly colored bath toys that will encourage imaginative play for infants include:

- Plastic animals, teethers, and waterproof rattles

Toddlers will enjoy the following:

- Doll clothes to "wash"
- Tea set
- Funnels
- Plastic tubes or straws to blow bubbles
- Watering cans
- Bath activity centers

Bathing Safety Tips

- *Never* leave your baby or child unattended in the tub. Remember: A baby can drown in a small amount of water.
- Have all your supplies—towels, toiletries, diapers, fresh clothing—within reach so you will not have to leave your baby alone.
- Take the phone off the hook so that you won't be distracted.
- Fill the tub before undressing the baby.
- Always test the water before putting a baby/child in the tub. Testing the water with your hand will mislead you. If you don't have a water thermometer, test the water with your foot.
- For good hygiene, wash the cleaner areas such as the head, trunk, arms, back, and feet first, then wash the genital area. Use a different washcloth for the genital area (keeping a special-color washcloth only for the genital area will make it easier to remember).
- When child is old enough to use the bathtub, use a bath mat or stick-on grids to prevent slipping.
- Always turn the cold water spigot off last so that the faucet will not be too hot if your child should touch it.

- Plastic containers or empty shampoo bottles
- Kitchen utensils (pots and pans, strainers, egg beaters, measuring cups, spoons, etc.)

Gum in Hair

One day, your child may come to you with gum in his hair. There are at least three ways to deal with this frequently humorous and always exasperating situation:

- Rub peanut butter in hair and gum and remove with tissue. Wash.
- Freeze hair with ice cubes and peel gum off hair.
- Rub cold cream in hair and pull down on strands of hair with dry towel.

Diapers Now, Get Ready!

Whether you use a diaper service, wash cloth diapers at home, buy disposable diapers, or a combination of those options, you're going to be making lots of changes. Newborns go through approximately 100 diapers a week. Toddlers need approximately 50 diapers per week. So plan on becoming knowledgeable about diapers.

Cloth Diapers

Cloth diapers are 100 percent cotton. They come in bird's-eye, a tightly woven fabric that is soft, absorbent, and expensive, or gauze, an open-weave fabric that tends to be less absorbent.

Cloth diapers are sold either contoured (shaped to the baby's bottom), prefolded (folded and stitched into place, with several layers in the center), or flat (a double layer of unfolded fabric). You'll need to buy 5 dozen if you plan to wash twice a week.

The advantages of using cloth diapers are that they are cheaper than disposable diapers, especially if you do your own laundry, and they are reliable, soft, and comfortable. You can also use them for other purposes such as protection when burping the baby, or as a protective cover over sheets in the crib or carriage.

The disadvantages of using cloth diapers have to do with their inconvenience. They are not convenient when traveling or visiting, and not as easy to put on a baby as disposable diapers. Cloth diapers require diaper pails—and patience!

A diaper service adds to your expense, but can be a big help if you use cloth diapers. Diaper services are labor-saving, guarantee sterilized cloth, and pick up and deliver to your home. Most diaper services provide the diapers, and a diaper pail.

Although home-laundered diapers are the least expensive, remember you have to add the cost of detergents and electricity to run washer and dryer to overall cost. You have to rinse all soiled diapers, soak diapers in a diaper pail with water and detergent, and run them through a rinse cycle in your washing machine before you wash them in mild soap, using the hottest cycle on your washing machine.

Cloth Diaper Safety Tips

- Don't buy diaper pins with plastic top designs. The plastic tops can chip off.
- When pins get dull, throw them away. Most pinning accidents happen when using a dull pin and more pressure is applied to push the pin through the diaper.
- Always place fingers between pin and baby when diapering to prevent stabbing the baby.
- Make sure the pail has two locks—one for the pail and one for the deodorizing compartment.
- Buy pins with metal safety caps on the heads, which prevent accidental opening.

Disposable Diapers

Disposable diapers are comparatively expensive and not as soft as cloth diapers, but they are so convenient, you'll want to consider them. Just keep these hints in mind:

- Look for the softest and thickest brand.
- Don't use brands that shred or that can be pulled apart easily. The baby can choke on the pieces.
- Try to locate a store that discounts disposable diapers. Large discount toy stores often discount diapers.

The Changing Area

Organize the baby's clothing, hamper, diaper pail, or trash can with top for soiled diapers near the area you plan on changing the baby. Also keep baby's toiletries near the changing area; at least keep them together on a tray, so in one swoop you can find all the supplies you need for changing your baby:

- Diapers
- Disposable wipes
- Baby powder
- Baby lotion
- Petroleum jelly
- Cotton swabs
- Masking tape (comes in handy when the tape on the disposable diapers does not stick)
- Ointment for diaper rash (check with your pediatrician)

The golden rule is to work fast. Babies don't like being changed and toddlers don't like lying down and remaining still. Distraction works sometimes. Try talking and singing (see pages 179–182 for lullabies and rhymes). Have a toy mirror, toys, mobiles, and books nearby for baby to play with.

Other Diaper-Changing Rules

- Change baby often.
- Wash baby's bottom with warm water and mild soap or disposable wipes. Use different color washcloth for baby's bottom so that you can distinguish from cloths used for other parts of the baby's body.
- For greater absorbency at night, double diapers.
- To avoid being sprayed with urine, cover a boy baby's penis when changing his diaper.

Diaper Rash

Most babies get some form of diaper rash because they have sensitive skin. If it persists, consult your pediatrician by phone for recommendations. You might want to discuss with her/him changing the brand of diapers and detergent, or ointment you use. If you are using a diaper service, inform your service representative of the rash. He or she might have some suggestions for a different type of cloth diaper for your baby.

More Diapering Safety Tips

- *Never* leave your baby unattended on the changing table or changing area.
- Keep supplies for changing near enough to reach so you don't leave the baby unattended, but out of the baby's reach or the curiosity of a roaming toddler.
- Always throw away paper pull tabs from diapers.
- Regardless of what type diapers you use, all feces should be emptied into the toilet. Throwing out a soiled disposable diaper containing the baby's feces can present serious public health problems.
- The best method of throwing away a soiled paper diaper is to roll it tightly so that the soiled area is not exposed to air. Put it in a plastic bag and tie, then put the bag in a receptacle that has a plastic garbage bag. Tie the bag tightly when you dispose of it.

Toilet Training

Toilet training should be a natural and unpressured experience for your child. A child will benefit from learning at her own pace when she is physically and emotionally ready, as your pediatrician will probably assure you.

Is Your Child Ready?

Professionals recommend beginning toilet training around the beginning or middle of your child's second year. There are several general signs of readiness:

- When your child is able to understand and follow simple directions.

- The diapers stay dry for a couple of hours.
- There is good muscle control.
- Your child seems interested in becoming more independent and in acting grown-up.

Children are easier to train in warm weather because they have fewer clothes to remove. But don't begin toilet training under stressful situations such as major changes in the child's life (moving, new baby, divorce, etc.), or when your child is going through a negative stage. Once you start, be patient. Children tend to make mistakes during toilet training in new situations, when they are absorbed in play, or when they are very excited or feeling sick.

Bowel control is accomplished before urine control and waking control before sleeping control. Staying dry at night or during naptime is not part of toilet training, but is accomplished later on.

Are You Ready?

During toilet training, when your child tells you he has to go to the potty, you have to stop what you are doing and take your child to the bathroom. If you are away from home, you'll have to find a bathroom. Often, you'll be in the car, or store, or waiting at the cashier line in the supermarket when your child needs to go. Your life will have to change for a while. So don't begin to train your child if you are feeling tired or pressured.

Preparing for Toilet Training

- Discuss your ideas and plans with your pediatrician.
- Read books on toilet training.
- *Remember* the words that you select for toilet-associated words will be used a long time by your child. Using the word *bubbles* for *urine* may sound cute for your baby tot, but not be practical at nursery school when your child states he wants to make bubbles and the teacher brings out some Ivory liquid soap.
- Try to gain a sense of your child's toileting schedule. See if there is a general pattern that you could work with when you begin your toilet training.
- Read special books about toilet training to your child. One special book is *No More Diapers* by Joan Brooks (Dell, 1982). A story about a little girl and a little boy and their toilet-training experiences. The book also includes instructions and suggestions for

parents. For other reading materials, see bibliography in the Appendix.

- Involve your child in the selection of the toilet training equipment. You decide on the model and let your child select the color or design painted on the seat.
- Buy special underpants that are colorful or have special TV characters printed on the material. Buy oversized pants so that the pants are easier to pull up and down.

No matter which method or plan you decide upon, remember that the training is an ongoing process. It will take time, patience, and a lot of love and support. With this kind of understanding, your child will gain the important feelings of self-esteem and self-worth while passing through this developmental stage.

Toilet-Training Equipment

One option is an adapter to the adult toilet. It is lightweight and there is no need to wash any parts after using because the urine and feces go directly into the toilet. However, some children may fear the height, falling into the water, or the loud flushing sound of the adult toilet. You will also need to assist your child on and off the seat until he can negotiate it comfortably himself. Eventually you will need a footstool to allow the child to seat himself.

When buying the adapter model, check that all the edges are rounded and smooth. The catches that hold the seat to the adult toilet should be made of rubber to prevent damage to the adult seat. The guards that are provided on the adapter model for training boys to divert their urine can be dangerous as little boys climb on and off the toilet seat. Don't use the guards.

Another option is a floor model child-sized potty, usually made of molded plastic. It is easy for the child to use and can be moved. Most models can separate so the top of the seat can be used as an adapter to the adult toilet. The only negative is that you have to empty and clean the receptacle. Select one that has a wide base, that is stable and not easy to tip over. See that the edges are smooth and the receptacle under the seat should be removed from the top rather than from the rear. When selecting the potty, take your child with you and have him try out the model you prefer.

CHAPTER **3**

Furniture that "Grows" with Your Child

Just like babies themselves, baby furniture is small, cute and irresistible. However, selecting furniture for the nursery should be based on growing needs of your baby rather than on appearances.

When my husband and I shopped for our first nursery, I had a mental picture of the two of us looking down into a lovely wicker bassinet—but not much information on practicality and safety requirements. So we chose a highly recommended store where we felt we could put our trust in the salesman.

"You start with the crib first," he informed us. Before we knew it, we were the proud owners of a crib, standard mattress and bumpers, a dresser/changing table, toy chest, and crib-side lamp, all in the same cheery Raggedy Ann-and-Andy motif. We congratulated ourselves that the wall-to-wall carpeting in the baby's room was just the right shade of blue to complement the colorful red, yellow, and blue furniture.

It took just a few months to realize how we had been led astray by Ann and Andy—not to mention the furniture salesman. The large, deep toy box had a way of "hiding" favorite toys and "losing" parts to toys, and there was always a danger of its lid falling down on Erik's fingers. We didn't have anywhere to store books, toiletries, and other baby-related paraphernalia. Even the lamp became a hazard when Erik learned to use it for mountain-climbing practice. And the pretty blue carpeting wasn't so pretty after daily assaults by spit-up, Cheerios, and leaky diapers. Eventually the carpeting frustrated Erik, as he tried to play on the carpet with his cars and blocks. He needed a flat surface for that kind of play.

Finally, when Erik was around 2 years old and had outgrown the

29

crib and we were in desperate need of additional storage space, I shopped again for beds and dressers. There was absolutely nothing in the stores that went with the changing table/dresser we had bought at the end of my first pregnancy, so we had to start from scratch with a new set of dressers.

I wish we had known that there are three major changes in a child's living space: the nursery (newborn to 2 years), the playroom-bedroom (2½ to 6 years), and the workroom-bedroom (7 years and up).

So, the question is: Do you want a traditional nursery in which furnishings are functional only for the first 2 to 3 years, or a baby's room in which the furniture is appropriate through the teen years? The answer will depend on your taste, budget, and the time you have available for shopping. If you want the furniture you buy to make transitions smoothly, keep the following tips in mind:

1. **Everything in its place.** Children acquire *tremendous* amounts of clothing, toys, books, records, sports equipment, and more. You'll need plenty of storage space that makes it easier to find, display, and put away these precious possessions.
2. **Little things mean a lot.** Buy furniture for practicality—and let colorful accessories (sheets, quilts, pictures, curtains, and toys) create a cheerful atmosphere, which is age-appropriate.
3. **Washable—or else!** Look for furniture that wipes clean instantly. You should be able to remove spills, paint, crayons, and Magic Markers easily. (Don't forget to ask salespeople what you should use for daily cleaning.)

The Nursery

The First Steps in Planning

Although some parents prefer to wait until after their newborn comes home from the hospital, many begin planning their child's nursery during the last trimester. Setting up a nursery can be a wonderful project for the whole family, and there is a wide range of furniture and decor to choose from, for all tastes and budgets. Here's what you'll need:

A place to sleep
A place to dress and diaper
Storage space for clothes, toys, and toiletries

Where to Begin

You can start familiarizing yourself with bedroom furniture by visiting stores or looking at catalogs. Bedroom furniture is manufactured in collections of items such as cabinets, dressers, bureaus, shelves, mirrors, beds, cribs, armoires, bookcases, vanities, desk sets, and so forth, which are made in various styles such as contemporary, modern, or Early American. Some of these collections will be modular, that is, made up of various components that can be arranged in interlocking combinations and updated and reorganized as a child's needs change.

Plan Ahead

If you do decide to buy a collection, you can start with two or three pieces for your newborn and add on as your child's needs change. You can always match different styles. You may like one collection's storage pieces but not its cribs.

Remember, you will only use the crib for approximately two years but the storage pieces could last until adulthood. Try to select storage pieces made by a well-established manufacturer, so that you're sure to be able to match them in the future.

If your local stores don't carry the style or pieces that you want, they may be able to give you catalogs to order from. Or call or write to the following manufacturers, who will tell you where to find the nearest retailers who carry their collections:

Bassett Furniture Industries
Main Street
Bassett, Virginia 24055
(703) 629-7511

Child Craft
Division of Smith Cabinet Mfg. Co.
P.O. Box 444
Salem, Indiana 47167
(812) 883-3111

Corrado Nursery Furniture Mfg. Co.
140 West 22nd Street
New York, NY 10011
(212) WA9-8575

Scandinavian Design
127 East 59th Street
New York, NY 10022
(212) 755-6078

Simmons Juvenile Products Company, Inc.
613 East Beacon Avenue
P.O. Box 287
New London, Wisconsin
(414) 982-2140

Williamsburg Furniture
Connor Forest Industries
330 Fourth Street
Wausau, Wisconsin 54401
(715) 842-0511

Let the Buyer Beware—Secondhand Furniture

You may prefer to furnish your nursery with furniture from family, friends, garage sales, resale shops, or classified ads. Whatever your source, always check with the U.S. Consumer Product Safety Commission Hotline—1-800-638-2772. They can tell you which models of furniture or equipment have been recalled by manufacturers. If possible, be ready with the name, serial number, and manufacturer of the product when you call. For a copy of their free booklet write to the United States Consumer Product Safety Commission, Nursery Equipment Buyer's Guide, Washington, D.C. 20207.

Now that you know what you like (and what to watch out for), you'll be ready to buy individual pieces.

Bassinet, Cradle, or Crib?

- A bassinet may be used for the first four months after birth, or until your baby becomes too active for such a small space. Cozy and portable, the bassinet must be sturdy and free from rough edges. Check to make sure all locks and latches are secure.
- A carriage that is easily separated from its frame can double as a bassinet.
- The cradle will rock, but it will also become too small in about four months. It usually can't be disassembled, and it's not easy to store. Again, make sure it's sturdy and can be locked if you can't resist its charm.
- The standard crib comes in a great variety of styles, and can be used from birth to about 2½ years.
- A Port-a-Crib is less expensive, and can be used until your child is 12 to 18 months old, depending on his size and activity level. It collapses easily for travel, but it's not as sturdy as the standard crib.
- A convertible crib later becomes a junior bed that can be used up to about age 5. It's smaller than a standard bed and more expensive than a regular crib.

Watch Out for These Hidden Hazards When You Shop:

- Crib slats should be no more than 2⅜ inches apart so that babies cannot slip through the slats and possibly be strangled.
- Metal hardware used on the crib must have no rough edges.
- Locks and latches on the dropside of a crib must be safe from accidental release or release by the baby inside the crib.
- Buy a crib with as large a distance as possible between the top of the side rail and the mattress support. Discourage baby from trying to climb out. For maximum protection against falls, the top of the side railing when raised should be at least 26 inches from the top of the mattress.
- Baby tends to teethe on the rails of the crib. Make sure that these rails are smooth and free of splinters.
- If possible, select a crib that has rounded slats rather than square ones because square bars have sharper edges, and are more likely to cause injury if baby falls into them.
- Watch out for cribs with plastic ornaments that can break.
- Give the crib a good shake. Does it seem sturdy?
- Is everything firmly attached?
- Is the paint on the crib nontoxic (without poisonous lead)?

*Snug and Safe—Tips for Using Cribs**

- As soon as your child is able to pull himself up to a standing position, set the mattress at its lowest point.
- Babies are intrepid rock climbers—don't leave toys in the crib where they may be used as stepping stones!
- The same goes for dangling objects. Never leave a toy on a string or a laundry bag within your little explorer's reach.
- Loose clothing can become entangled on the tops of bedposts.
- Replace any damaged teething rails. They can cut your child's mouth.
- A crib should not be used as a playpen.
- If the crib is placed near a window, make sure that there are no drapery or venetian blind cords within the child's reach.
- Your child is ready to "graduate" from his crib once the height of the side rail is less than three-fourths of his height.

*Recommended by the U.S. Consumer Product Safety Commission.

Accent on Color

At last, here comes the fun part—the accessories that brighten and personalize your child's room! Besides bumpers, sheets, quilt, and curtains, you can give the nursery a happy, colorful, upbeat atmosphere with all kinds of decorations you can buy or make yourself— *mobiles, wallpaper, murals, music boxes*, and *wall hangings*.

Rock-a-Bye Baby—and Parent!

You'll spend many hours just sitting with your newborn. Also feeding, playing, singing, comforting, and talking. The motion of a *rocking chair* will relax you both. Make sure it's a good "fit" for you, and don't forget to buy back and seat cushions.

Floors and Rugs

If you have bare floors in your nursery, place a throw rug near the crib to muffle the sound of dropping toys. Some portion of the floor should be uncovered for your child to play and build on. Wood or vinyl flooring with removable area rugs is ideal for your child's nursery.

Safety Tip

- Put a piece of rubber matting underneath area rugs to prevent slipping. Large bathroom rugs are great and machine washable.

Mattresses

- Bassinets and cradles come with specially sized mattresses. Port-A-Crib mattresses are available in two thicknesses. The thicker one is firmer and gives more support.
- For the crib, choose a quality mattress (innerspring is best) that will retain its firmness and resiliency and budget in other areas!
- Mattresses must fit snugly. If you can fit more than two fingers between the mattress and the crib, the mattress is too small.

Bumpers

They're runners of quilted fabric that tie or snap around the inside of the crib, bassinet, or cradle so your baby can't bump against the sides or get wedged between the bars. They are available in a variety of sizes and materials, but plastic is preferable for crib use because it is easier to clean and provides the greatest safety. Bumpers should tie or snap around the inside of the crib in at least six places. Trim off any excess length from straps, so your baby can't chew on it or become entangled. Remove crib bumpers when your baby begins to pull up to a standing position. She can stand on the bumpers and fall out of the crib, or can fall within the crib, hitting her face against the bars.

Making the Crib*

You'll need:

A quilted mattress pad in standard or Port-A-Crib size
Fitted sheets, ditto
A blanket or comforter (washable)
A dry-down—which is a piece of waterproof material that protects the sheets from accidents
Cloth diaper

Now fit the quilted pad over the mattress. Add a full-length dry-down and pull the fitted sheet over both. Then place a small dry-down across the end of the crib, over the sheet. Finally cover the dry-down with a cloth diaper. (This method works just as well for protecting carriage, bassinet, or cradle linen.)

For Dressing and Changing

A changing table consists of a waterproof changing pad, a safety strap, and a space to store clothes and toiletries. You'll need it from birth until about age 2. It should be sturdy and at a comfortable working height for you (probably waist level).

Some models can be converted to a bookcase/dresser later on. Make sure that the manufacturer makes other matching pieces of furniture that you can add as needed.

A changing pad can be used instead of a changing table. It is an

*Technique recommended by the American Red Cross.

inexpensive vinyl pad that you can use anywhere. It just doesn't provide a place to store clothing and toiletries!

Storage Furniture

- Children will need four to six drawers for their clothes up until age 5. Children 6 years and up need six to eight drawers.
- Small drawers will come in handy for storing belts, socks, ribbons, mittens, barrettes, and jewelry.
- At least 6 to 12 inches of space will be taken up with toy storage.
- Children use about 3 feet of shelf space for books, allowing at least 1 foot in height for oversized picture books.
- Dresser drawers should slide easily, with knobs at a height that your child can reach without straining. And if the dresser is 21 to 26 inches tall, the top surface can be used as a work surface when she's older. Drawers should be "no pull" or have knobs so your child can't catch her fingers in the handles.
- The armoire can be a good deal, giving you lots of storage in exchange for very little floor space. It's a cabinet placed on top of a three-drawer base. The doors at the top open onto shelves that can be converted to hanging space with a clothes bar.
- The chifforobe is a side-by-side arrangement, with four drawers on one side and a cabinet with either shelves (sold separately) or hanging space on the other. It's smaller than the armoire, but you can put a changing pad on top of the dresser part.
- For odds and ends, choose from cubes, cubbies, and lockers. And for super-efficient storage, consider a wall unit—purchased, do-it-yourself, or architect-designed—built into a walk-in closet or cabinet.

Let There Be Light

- Table lamps can be cute, but present hazards for the curious child. They also take up valuable surface space.
- Track lighting is expensive, but can be directed to different parts of the room, and it is way out of baby's reach.
- Put a dimmer on the switch for ceiling light fixtures. Newborns can't turn over if the bright light is bothering them. The dimmer can be used as a night light that makes nighttime feedings easier and is reassuring to small children in a dark room.
- No extension cords! Adventurous babies may follow them to their source.
- *Be sure all bulbs are covered and outlets capped.*

Around the House— Swings, Walkers, Jumpers, Playpens

It has been said that parents of infants need two or three pairs of hands, especially when the baby is restless and housework must be done or dinner has to be made. At times such as these, an infant seat, playpen, walker, or jumper can come in handy. Remember, however, that your baby must be closely supervised in them.

When my first son, Erik, was a baby, I made use of many inanimate "mother's helpers." I set up a playpen in the dining room so I could watch Erik while I was in the kitchen. I had a mechanical swing in my bedroom and used an infant seat when I was working in other parts of the house. And Erik loved motion, so when he became fretful, or on the long days when it was raining or too cold to go out, I used the swing, a jumper, and a walker.

Swings, walkers, and jumpers are useful—but dispensable—items. They tend to be expensive, considering the relatively brief time they are in use. And you can also use a baby carrier, carriage, or stroller for many of the same purposes.

Swings

Swings can be used from 1 month to 1 year. Check individual manufacturer's suggestions for use by child's weight and age.

Never Leave Baby Unattended in Equipment!

Infant Seats

Infant seats can be used from birth to when baby can sit up by himself, around 5 to 6 months. They are usually made of plastic with a plastic pad and safety strap. The seat has several positions, from reclining to sitting. Because the newborn is unable to hold his or her head up, the infant seat provides the infant with an opportunity to explore his surroundings from a reclining position. As the infant gains greater control of his head, the seat can be adjusted more toward a seating position. When the infant starts eating solid food, he or she can be fed in the infant seat. Because of its many uses, the infant seat is a helpful piece of equipment. *However, you must use the infant seat with caution.*

What to Look For in Buying an Infant Seat

- Is the seat sturdy, or can it tip over easily?
- Is the base wider than the seat?
- Do the seat-adjustment mechanisms hold securely?
- Is the base made of a nonslippery material?
- Are there any sharp edges?
- Is the seat equipped with a sturdy restraining device? The straps should be made out of a strong material and capped with a firmly holding buckle. One strap should fasten around the waist and there should be a connecting crotch strap so the infant can't slide out feet first.

Safety Tips on Infant Seats from the Consumer Product Safety Commission

- Never leave baby unattended in an infant seat.
- Never put an infant seat on the edge of a pedestal table or on a high, smooth surface where the baby's motion could propel the seat off the side.
- Always use the safety straps.
- Never use an infant seat as a car seat.

Walkers

Walkers can be used from age 6 months (or when the baby can sit unassisted) to around 9 months. Check for each model the recommended weight.

A walker does *not* teach the baby to walk, although some children love it because it gives a prewalking child freedom to move. Be aware that the walker is not a sturdy piece of equipment; it can be tipped easily. So your baby needs close supervision while in one.

Jumpers

Jumpers can be used from age 4 months to 8 months.

In a jumper a baby is suspended with toes just touching the ground. Rubber cables or springs enable the baby to move up and down by pushing with the toes.

Some babies love it; others may be scared. All babies need close supervision while in jumpers.

Playpens

Playpens are used from age 3 months to 9 months or longer, depending on your baby's tolerance for being enclosed. A playpen provides a relatively safe place to put the baby for short periods. If living space is large, a playpen keeps a baby confined to a particular area. You can do without a playpen, of course, if you childproof a specific area and use gates to confine the baby to that part of the house.

Things to Look For When Selecting a Playpen

- The netting should be fine so baby can't climb on mesh or get buttons from clothing caught.
- There should be thick padding around bars, on corners, and around top of playpen.
- Flooring should be secure and plastic padding on bottom should be strong and thick.
- Hinges should be guarded so baby cannot maneuver them.

Safety Tip

- Warning: Don't leave side of a playpen down. Baby can smother in the mesh that collects on the floor of the playpen.

The Preschooler's Bedroom

Between your child's second and third year, the nursery grows up, too, and becomes a bedroom. This is the start of the "me" years, when kids start to develop feelings about "my own room." What was once just a place to sleep becomes a place to play, alone or with friends.

Before you make any major changes, think about what this more active, newly independent person needs. It's a time when a child's imagination really begins to soar, so the decoration and arrangement of the room should encourage lots of creative play. And don't forget, your baby's not a baby any more. You can help your child do a lot for himself by making it easy to find and reach his own clothes, books, and toys. And now's a great time to teach him that everything has its place—and it's *not* the middle of the floor!

Try a theme! Planning accessories around an idea for fantasy play is a fun way to organize the room *and* stimulate your child's imagination. How about stars, clouds, and rainbows? Or space travel, the seashore, mountains, a forest, a market, or fairytale characters! Make it happen with "theme" linens, murals, posters, pillows, a bulletin board (good for "exhibitions" of your child's own artwork), indoor climbing equipment, cardboard playhouses/stores/rockets, or even a whole blackboard wall (make it yourself with blackboard paint).

Her First Bed

Years ago, many parents purchased youth beds (33 × 66 inches) as a transition from a crib before buying a twin bed (39 × 75 inches). Today, most children are moved directly from a crib to a twin bed, eliminating the youth bed. If necessary, portable guard rails can be put on a twin bed as a safety measure. Make sure any bed you buy is movable and washable.

Some Options for Beds

- Buy a good twin-size mattress and put it on the floor. This arrangement makes a nice transition from a crib to a bed. When you want to buy a bed, you already have the mattress. The

mattress on the floor also makes a wonderful place to play, tumble around, or snuggle up with a favorite toy.
- Canopy beds are special treats for your little princess. It's a good idea if the posts are removable. Your child might want a canopy bed at age 5 but not at 14. Canopy beds can be real dust collectors.
- Headboard, box spring, and frame are options, not necessities!
- A day bed is an excellent choice if your child's room has other functions for the family.
- A trundle bed saves space. Two children can sleep in the space of one bed because one bed pulls out. Great for when your child has a friend sleeping over.
- A captain's bed has storage drawers underneath. Perfect if space for dressers and cabinets is limited.
- Bunk beds are great for sleeping, playing, and privacy. Look for the kind that can also be used separately and are easy to move. A ladder or steps for climbing down should be part of the structure. Guard rails should run the full length of the upper bunk. The top bunk should not be used for sleeping until the child is 7 years old.

Selecting a Mattress

There are two basic types of mattresses: the innerspring and the urethane foam. Hair block mattresses are available, but many lack the resiliency of the foam and innerspring models. Also remember that young children love to jump and bounce around on their mattress. A foam mattress is less likely to be ruined by an active child. You might choose to buy a urethane foam mattress for a young child and then purchase a good quality innerspring mattress when your child is about 9 years old.

Making Your Child's Bed

Many children who can keep dry during the day continue to wet their bed at night. After you put the mattress cover on, always put a large cotton dry-down over the mattress. Buy two or three, because they will come in handy. I also used to put a smaller dry-down sheet between the comforter and fitted sheet, so if my son had an accident I only had to change the dry-down and his pj's, not the sheet.

Simplify Bed Making

To simplify bed making, use a fitted sheet for the bottom and a warm, washable quilt or comforter instead of a top sheet and blanket. This method saves laundry, and it is especially good if your child is sleeping on a mattress on the floor. Even 5-year-olds can make their own beds this way.

Selecting Sheets and Comforters/Blankets

Bedding featuring Disney and Sesame Street figures, Smurfs, the "Peanuts" gang, and so forth make a bed seem more personal to a young child who is not fully adjusted to a bed. There are many fitted sheets and pillow cases with these designs. If you like patterned sheets, buy a solid color blanket or comforter that can blend with a variety of other colors. Put off buying a bedspread until your child is older (around 9 years).

Additional Furniture

- Table and chairs will get a lot of use. Around 2½ years, your child will enjoy sitting down to play at a small table. If you are on a tight budget, save your money and buy a better desk when your child is older and needs an area for doing homework and hobbies. Your child will be perfectly satisfied working and playing on your kitchen table or on the floor. I used to put one of the thick dining table mats on the floor for Erik and Marc when they wanted to color.

  If you decide to buy a table and chair set, select sturdy furniture that doesn't tip easily, especially the chairs. In addition, look for furniture that is easy to clean. You should be able to wipe off spills, paint, crayons, and Magic Markers.

- Floor-length mirror is an important play element in your child's room. They love to look at themselves and interact with their mirror image.

Flooring

The floor doesn't have to change much now, if your nursery was better planned than ours. You still need a warm, easy-to-clean, nonslip surface that's smooth and flat enough for all kinds of play. The best "growing-along" solution is wood or vinyl flooring with washable area rugs backed with rubber matting.

Lighting

Again, no changes here. Track lighting is still the safest and smartest. A dimmer switch makes it easier to look in without waking your sleeping beauty.

Clothing Storage for Your "I'll-Do-It-Myself" Kid

- The clothing rack in the closet should be at your child's height.
- Use scaled-down children's hangers.
- Put knobs and hooks on the inside door of the closet for pajamas, coats, and hats.
- Hang a shoe bag on the other side of the closet door for shoes, boots, mittens, and scarves.
- Use plastic boxes and drawer dividers to keep piles of clothing near, and to make things easier to find.

A Place to Play

By the time a child turns 3, the quality of his play and types of toys change. Toys now come in sets and have lots of accessories.

As they emerge from toddlerhood, children need a different kind of space for playing. Rather than the roving space that your toddler required, 2½-year-olds begin to settle down in their play. They might like to set up a space with blocks, dolls, or tea cups, or trucks and workmen. And because they may stop playing for a while and then return later to play, it is important that they have a play space that is solely theirs. The space can be in his or her room or a corner of another room.

Storing Toys, Books, and Puzzles

The toys should be an integral part of the play space. Because many accessories from various play sets are interchangeable, you can store similar items together (all the cars together, all the people together, all the animals together, all the furniture together). You can store the toys in open containers such as cubbies, cubes, trays, baskets, Lucite or plastic drawers. The open containers allow your child to see what toys are where. Some containers can be stacked one on top of the other. When you put the containers on a shelf or stack them, tape a picture and the name of the type of toys to the container. This visual clue makes the toys more accessible to your child.

Puzzle racks are reasonably priced, take up little space, and can easily hold five to ten puzzles.

Keep about five to ten books "in circulation" in a specific place. You can put the others away and change the books each week. Be sure to place the "circulating" books face out so that your child can tell what the book is about.

Fostering Creativity and Independence in Play

Organize play space into "subject areas":

- *Quiet area*—Here's where your child will read or listen to records or tapes. Toss a few pillows around and always leave out a few books "in circulation." This should be a cozy, comfortable space.
- *Arts and crafts area*—For drawing, coloring, cutting, and pasting, there should be a flat surface (worktable, dresser top, or a mat on the floor) with a shelf nearby that holds crayons, markers, paper, and other supplies.
- *Building area*—On flat, smooth floor space, stocked with scraps of material, markers, paper, and tape. And there should be enough room to leave the finished product up for a while.
- *Area for dramatic play*—Plenty of space and fantasy decorations for playing with dolls, putting on shows, playing house, and anything else your child can imagine.

CHAPTER 4

Smart Clothing Choices

Sometimes it's the shirt with the rabbits. Or the shirt *without* the rabbits. Children as young as 2 years old may have very definite style and color preferences, or favor certain fabrics or textures. If your child is not comfortable or dislikes a piece of clothing, you will have a struggle on your hands, whether it's with a squirming 6-month-old or a screaming 6-year-old. When it happens—and it *will*—think how you would feel.

The first and last time you will have complete control over what your child wears is when you select...

The Layette—Clothing and Linen

... because you buy it before your baby is born! The time to shop for a complete wardrobe for your newborn is during your last trimester of pregnancy. You don't even have to lug it home: most stores will not process the order until the baby is born. Then you can either pick up the layette or have it delivered.

Avoid (Some) Growing Pains!

When you buy the layette, you will be in a nesting mood—and in a shop full of the smallest, cutest, cuddliest clothing you've ever seen. Resist! You're only buying for the next six to eight months at best. Pass up the 0-to-three-month size, and steer toward the six-month size. Most newborns won't get lost in it, and the clothes will be useful longer.

The Best-Dressed Baby

- Get overalls and "stretchies" with snaps at the crotch for quick changes.
- Babies hate to lie still or have things pulled over their heads. If clothing has too many buttons, snaps, or other fasteners, pass it by.
- Washability is key, for obvious reasons. *(Check the label for "wash before using" instructions.* If prewashing is required, use a mild detergent, such as Ivory Snow.)
- Newborns move around more than you might think, so don't buy frilly or constricting clothing, no matter how adorable.

Self-Indulgence

But do splurge on at least two incredibly cute outfits. After days, weeks, and months of sleepless nights, spit-up, and scattered cereal, you *need* and *deserve* to hear people gush and say, "Oh, how *cute!*"

Buntings

Buntings are sacklike outer garments with sleeves. They're easy to put on, but they don't work well with car seats, strollers, or frontpacks, because all of these contraptions have crotch straps.

Snow Bunnies

If yours is a winter baby, you'll need buntings and a *snowsuit*, all with hoods. Buy early, because unlike winter in a cold climate, these items disappear from the stores in January or February. You need a *hat*, too, because cold air still gets in through hoods. Most babies hate hats, so buy one that ties to keep your baby from pulling it off. (The ones that tie on the side of the chin tend to be more comfortable than the hats that tie underneath.)

For the Premature Baby

There *are* sizes to fit the premature baby, although the garments won't be labeled as such. Ask for newborn to three months (fits 0 to

12 pounds), extra small, instant fit clothing, or a European size 50 or 60. (Some other sizes, although labeled for full-term babies, actually are quite small.) Undershirts with ties or gowns with strings at the bottom tend to be one-size-fits-all.

With these clothing pointers in mind, you are ready for The List—of every piece of clothing and linen you'll need, and how many of each will make your life easiest. Take it shopping, and you'll have all the basics.

LINEN

Waterproof sheet for the crib (dry-down)	2
Fitted crib sheet, or fitted portable crib sheet, or fitted cradle or bassinet sheet	3–4
Receiving blanket (cotton flannel)	2
Blanket for the crib	1
Dry-down (puddle pad) for the crib	2
Terry cloth towel with hood or regular bath-size terry cloth towels; make sure they are soft and buy only white	2
Washcloths (buy some in another color to use for washing baby's bottom)	4
Cotton diapers (for protecting mother's clothes when feeding the baby and for protecting sheets in crib and carriage)	1 dozen
If you plan on using a carriage...	
Pad for the carriage (dry-down)	1
Fitted sheet for the carriage	2
Blanket for carriage	1

Fireproofing Clothing

The original fireproofing your child's garments were treated with only lasts up to 20 washings. You'll probably have to refireproof some items yourself—and it's a good idea to toss in curtains and other washable cloth decoration from the nursery at the same time. Here's a safe, easy formula*: Combine 9 ounces of Borax, 4 ounces of boric acid solution, and 1 gallon of warm water. Soak clean clothes or linens in this solution until it's completely absorbed. Dry as usual.

Now you have all the baby basics, but you'll find you can always use more/cuter/bigger/and *more* again of everything. Which brings us to...

Presents!

When people ask what you need, don't be shy. Give them specific ideas. And recommend stores you like, especially if they have a good exchange policy or if they pick up and deliver. Suggest size six months and up, so that friends and relatives get more chances to see their gift under actual wearing conditions. If you're not sure how much someone wants to spend, suggest *bibs, booties, fitted crib sheets, stretch suits*, or a multipocketed *cobbler's apron* for mom. All cost under $10.

Clothes for Ages 1 to 5

8 Months to 1½ Years

- As your baby gets more active, stretchies won't do anymore. Look for clothing that moves with your child: shirts, pants, dresses, and overalls.
- Crawling, walking, and falling are hard on clothing. Fight wear and tear with reinforced *double knees* (or attach iron-on patches to the insides of regular trouser knees).
- Babies this age are still "accident prone"—expect to change your child's clothes at least twice a day, and to need more bottoms than tops.

* From *The Mother's Almanac* by Marguerite Kelly and Elia S. Parsons (Doubleday, 1975).

CLOTHING

	When Baby Is Born			
	Spring	Summer	Fall	Winter
Snap undershirts				
size 3 months	2	2	2	2
size 6 months	4	4	4	4
(optional with disposable diapers) Waterproof pants— size 6 months	1 pr	1 pr	1 pr	1 pr
Stretchies (1 piece that snaps from head to toe)				
size 3 months	1	1	1	1
size 6 months	4	4	4	4
Kimonos (nightgown snaps at neck but opens down; flame-retardant fabric)	2	2	2	0
Gowns (drawstring at bottom)	2	2	2	2
Sweater and hat set	1	1	1	1
Blanket sleepers (zips down front—has arms but no fitted legs)	0	0	1	2
Snowsuit (usually 1 piece with arms and legs fitted)	1	1	1	1
Bunting (hooded bag with arms that zip up front or side)	0	0	1	1
Booties/Socks/Baby Slipper boots	2 pr	2 pr	2 pr	2 pr
Bib (can use cotton diapers)	2	2	2	2

- One-piece outfits (overalls, jumpers, dresses) are neater looking and warmer at this stage—little ones' bellies tend to stick out!
- Choose zippers and snaps—neither one of you will want to fuss with buttons. Also, children this age still hate to have things pulled over their heads, so make sure the neck of a pullover top stretches easily.

From 1½ to 3 Years

- This is when children start using clothes as props for imaginative play—and as places to store and collect things. Always empty pockets before washing!
- They're also fascinated by fasteners—buttons and snaps—and partial to pictures of favorite TV, book, or movie characters.
- Keep it simple—children who are just beginning to use the toilet need clothing that is easy to take off and put on again. (Elasticized waists are a lot safer than zippers or buttons!)

From 3 to 6 years

- Like toddlers, preschoolers prefer "do-it-myself" clothing, especially when they go to nursery school or to a friend's house. Overalls and things that fasten in the back are still too "advanced."
- Zippered coats and jackets are friendlier to little fingers than buttons.
- Gloves are still too tricky. Buy mittens (and clip to coat or jacket sleeves).
- Kids this age are more likely to get stains on shirts than pants, so now you'll need more tops than bottoms.
- Pants and tights will still tend to wear through at the knees, so stick with those iron-on patches and reinforced double knees.
- Thick-weave tights or professional dancing tights wear longest.
- When you take your 3-to-6-year-old shopping, cut down on wardrobe wrangles by offering a choice of two or three similar garments.
- And don't forget, school-going children have very definite ideas about what they have to have, and what they can't be seen in! Just in case the whole class switches from warm-up suits to Madonna minis, it's a good idea to buy just a few things at the beginning of each season. Then keep adding pieces as your child's tastes change and (you hope!) mature.

Basic Needs

You can keep your washing machine blessedly idle for up to four days at a stretch, if you have all the items on the following checklist.

6 to 8 pairs of underpants
6 to 8 pairs of undershirts
8 to 12 pairs of socks
3 to 4 pairs of pajamas
6 to 8 outfits
1 to 2 sweaters
1 sweat shirt (with zipper and hood)
1 raincoat with hood
1 rain hat
1 lightweight jacket for fall/spring
1 winter coat with hood
1 pair waterproof pants for snow (unless your child has a snowsuit)
2 winter hats
1 scarf
3 pairs mittens or gloves
1 pair slippers
1 pair boots for winter
1 pair of rain boots

OPTIONAL

bathrobe
belts
suspenders
umbrella
dress-up clothing, according to your family's needs
jogging suits

Shopping Tips for All Ages

- Watch out for labels that say "Hand Wash Only." Look for *machine washable/dryable* clothing.
- You may be an NFO (Natural Fibers Only) diehard, but don't forget that untreated 100 percent cotton needs ironing, whereas cotton/permanent press or knitted cotton doesn't.

- But cotton knit shirts usually shrink, so buy a bigger size than you think you'll need.
- Red is bright and cheerful—until you wash it and it bleeds all over everything else.
- *Socks* evaporate. Buy lots, in the same color and style, so they'll always match. (White is a color for all seasons—it goes with everything, and can be worn with shorts in summer.)
- Try to buy within a *color scheme*, so that everything matches. (Later on, it will save explaining *why* the lime-green shirt doesn't go with the red pants.)
- Buy several pairs of the same style *pajamas*. Then you can mix and match if a top or a bottom gets lost or soiled.
- Kids love *jogging suits* and pants. They are easy to put on, and they are multipurpose. Use them for daywear, to change into after school, or after a bath when it's still too early to put on pajamas.
- Check the underside of clothes to make sure that seams or the inner lining aren't scratchy.
- Buy *extra mittens* (same style and color) and an extra winter hat for that cold day when a mitten or hat gets lost, and the stores are already stocking nothing but bathing suits.
- *Coats* should be waterproof, and hooded. (Hoods don't disappear the way hats do.) Look for warmth without bulk—a down coat, although expensive, is lightweight, toasty warm and, unlike wool, acts as a wind breaker. (The higher the percentage of down, the warmer the coat will be.)
- Girls' heavy cabled tights make good *long underwear* for both girls and boys, up to about 5. By then, you can find long underwear made especially for boys.

Surviving the Shopping Trip

- Make a list—including your child's height, weight, and shoe size.
- Bring munchies if your child comes along. Good nonmessy snacks are vegetable sticks or sugarless gum. And don't forget a *collapsible cup* for the thirsty child who's too little to reach the store water fountains.
- Carry the snacks, cup, and such, in a *backpack*, so that you have two free hands. (You can also stuff kids' jackets in it, so you don't have to use your arms for coatracks.)
- Don't plan a shop-'til-you-drop marathon—consider your and your child's tolerance for going from store to store, trying things on, and waiting in line.

- For children under 2 you can buy by size (without trying on) and return when necessary.
- With preschoolers, you can shop during the least busy time, during school hours. Avoid Saturdays and holidays while you still can.
- If you're shopping with more than one child along, bring another adult if you can. This is a job for at least four grown-up hands and eyes!
- When you bring your child, and you find one or two styles that fit, write down the manufacturer's name and the style number, so you can go to another or larger store to buy the same style in several other colors or materials.
- Find a nearby store with an easy return policy—for cash, rather than for credit. Stock up on underwear, pajamas, and socks that you know will fit. Then select outfits to have your child try on at home.

Sale Strategies

When buying clothes for next winter or summer on sale, remember that kids' needs and tastes change a lot in a year. I once bought four pairs of Oshkosh overalls in the next size up, thinking they'd be great for the fall when Marc started nursery school. He *hated* them—away from home for the first time, he wanted clothes he could manage by himself! But if you plan ahead, sales can be a terrific source of useful, stylish, and *inexpensive* clothing.

- Call up your favorite store, or that expensive place where you'd love to find a special outfit and ask about their general or special sales. Ask to be put on their mailing list.
- For fall/winter clothes, expect sales around the first and second week in January. Some large department stores have prewinter sales in August.
- For spring/summer clothes, look for sales around Memorial Day.

Getting the Right Fit

Know the right size, and you'll waste less time with try-ons and returns. The following guidelines were developed by the garment industry and the National Bureau of Standards. However, you may find that your child is a perfect size 4 with one manufacturer but "grows" to a 6 with another! Make sure clothing has some give to it—children can grow amazingly fast, even in as little as two weeks. When using the following size charts:

for infants and babies—double the age in months to find the right size
for all other sizes—buy one size larger than your child's age

There is some overlap among the various groups of sizes:

Babies' size 18 months is similar to Toddler size 1
Babies' size 24 months is similar to Toddler size 2
Babies' size 36 months is similar to Toddler size 3
Toddlers' size 2 is similar to Children's size 2
Toddlers' size 3 is similar to Children's size 3
Toddlers' size 4 is similar to Children's size 4

European manufactured children's clothing tends to fit slimmer children. Also, undershirts run *very, very* small. Buy them larger than regular shirts.

Laundry

I didn't think about laundry much before I had children. Everything went in the weekly wash. Children's clothing is tougher: with one of my sons, all I had to do was look at his shirt and I could tell everything he'd eaten and done that day.

Children tend to be harder on their clothing just by being kids. They start out with "accident" and spit-up stains on clothes and sheets, then move right along to grass and dirt stains, and "wearing" chocolate ice cream, sticky red lollypops, and a rainbow of crayon marks on blouses and shirts. With so many different kinds of stains, it's no longer enough just to throw it into the washing machine and hope for the best. The following suggestions will come in handy.

Keeping Clothes Cleaner, Neater, Longer

- Make sure stains are removed before putting clothes in the dryer— heat sets stains *forever*.
- Soak colored clothes in cold water with a little white (distilled) vinegar to prevent dyes from running.
- To prevent wrinkling, fold or hang clothes as soon as they're dry.

SOCK SIZE CHART

Remember that socks sizes can vary
with individual brands.

Shoe Size	Sock Size
0	3½
1	4
1–2	4½
2½–3½	5
4–5	5½
5½–6½	6
7–8	6½
8½–9½	7
9½–10½	7½
11–12	8
12½–1½	8½
2–3½	9
4–5½	9½
6–6½	10
7–7½	10½

- Wash dark-colored clothes inside out to keep right sides from collecting lint.
- Turn corduroys inside out to wash.
- *Always check pockets before washing.*
- Close zippers and fasten hooks to prevent snags.
- To "dewrinkle" corduroys and velvet, tumble dry for 15 minutes with a damp towel.
- Add baking soda diluted in water to the rinse cycle to get rid of sour smells.
- Club soda will break up many stubborn stains. Rub it in.
- Spray starch prevents dirt from getting ground into the knees of pants.
- To clean rain slickers, sprinkle baking soda on soiled areas and gently rub it in with a damp cloth. Then wipe off with a wet sponge.
- Cut down on button-sewing time by using long-lasting, heavy-duty #8 thread.
- Always make a double knot at each end of drawstrings. If it gets pulled out anyway, wet the drawstring and put it in the freezer for a few minutes. When it gets stiff, it will be much easier to insert.
- To clean sneakers, wash alone in washing machine. Take out laces and tie to one hole. *Air dry only.*
- For no-pull knits, turn wash-and-dry tights, shirts, and jogging suits inside out before washing.

REMOVING STAINS

Type of Stain	Cleaning Directions
Baby food	Soak for a few hours in: 1 cup bleach 1 cup dishwasher liquid detergent 2 to 3 gallons of water then wash as usual.
Formula	Rub a paste of unseasoned meat tenderizer on stains. Roll the clothes up. Wait a few minutes before washing.

REMOVING STAINS (*cont.*)

Spit-up	Apply a paste of baking soda and water to fabric before washing.
Gum on clothing	Freeze garment; gum should flick off. Soak in white vinegar before washing. Soften with egg white; then scrape off and wash.
Crayons	Put stained area between clean paper towels or pieces of a brown paper bag; then press with a warm iron.
Vomit	Soak in cold water and then sponge with the following solution: 1 quart of warm water 1 tablespoon ammonia 1½ teaspoon liquid detergent Wash and rinse with baking soda in water (gives a fresh smell).
Egg	Soak stained clothing in cold water before laundering.
Grimy socks	Soak with a solution of baking soda and warm water. OR Boil in water with a slice of lemon.
Grass	Sponge with a water and vinegar solution; then rinse and wash as usual. OR Sponge with a water and denatured alcohol solution; then rinse and wash as usual.
Blood	Dab with hydrogen peroxide, then soak in cold water, scrub with soap or detergent, rinse with cold water. Wash as usual.
Mud	Let dry, then brush well and soak in cold water. If stain persists, rub a little detergent into it, and then rinse. Wash as usual.

REMOVING STAINS (*cont.*)

Chocolate	Sponge with cold water, if stain persists, soak in the following solution:
	    3 tablespoons of borax to
	    3½ cups of warm water
	Rinse and wash as usual.

Ice-cream Milk	Soak in cold water and then wash with water and soap or detergent. Rinse. If stain persists, sponge with safe cleaning fluid.
Urine	Soak in a solution of distilled white vinegar and water. Rinse and wash as usual.
Fruit juices Fruits Berries	Do not use soap! Stretch material over a large bowl and pour boiling water through stain. If stain persists, use bleach if safe for fabrics or use bleach substitute (see page 61). Then wash as usual.
Candy	Soak in warm water. If stain persists, add a few drops of distilled white vinegar and denatured alcohol to water. Then wash as usual.
Mustard	Sponge with a little hydrogen peroxide, or distilled white vinegar. Wash as usual.
Grease	Sprinkle some talcum, salt, or cornstarch on spot. Place stain face down on paper towels and go over the back with full-strength liquid detergent, using a clean white cloth. Then wash as usual.
Red candy	For stubborn red stains, soak with liquid laundry detergent, water, and a little bleach if material can take it. Wash as usual.
Tempera paint	Soak in warm water with liquid laundry detergent. Wash as usual.

> ## For all "no-bleach" fabrics:
>
> Add 1 to 1½ cups of distilled white vinegar
> to
> 1 gallon of water

For More Good Ideas:

Help! From Heloise (Avon, 1982).
Hints from Heloise (Avon, 1981).
Mary Ellen's Best of Helpful Hints (Warner, 1981).
The Family Circle Hints Book by Erika Douglas (Times Books, 1982).
Best Bets for Babies by Brooke Beebe (Dell, 1981).

Footwear

Know Your Shoe Stores

Look for stores where the salespeople are trained to fit young children. Just as all clothing in your child's usual size won't always fit, the same goes for shoes. Here are some things to think about the next time you buy shoes for your child:

- Is the store busy? Parents can only be fooled once, and won't come back if their children's shoes weren't well-fitted.
- The salespeople should be patient, and not rush either you or your child.

Fitting Children's Shoes: The Basic Procedure

Measure the length and width of both feet. If they're different, fit shoes to the larger size. Your child should be standing up when measured, because feet spread in a standing position.

How to Tell if the New Shoe Fits

The salesperson should check for fit in several places: width, length, girth, and ankle. It's also important to make sure the top front of the shoe "breaks" in the right place when your child is walking. There should be ½ to ⅔ inches of toe room to allow for growth.

Fashions for Little Feet

Never buy shoes that your child doesn't like, because it will be a continuous battle to get him to wear them. Keep trying on different styles until you find one that fits your child's tastes as well as his feet. If the salesperson loses patience, put the old shoes back on and walk— to another store!

How to Tell if Shoes Still Fit

You may be in luck—check every few months, using these guidelines:

- Make sure there's still room in the toe area.
- Look for redness or irritation on your child's feet.
- See if there's a toe mark on the side of the shoe.

If you're still not sure, it's time for a trip to the shoe store anyway, to ask the experts.

Baby's First Shoes

Your baby won't need shoes until she starts walking, but they're awfully cute. So, if you succumb...

- Be sure the salesperson is trained to fit babies.
- Look for flexible, lightweight shoes, such as the Stride Rite pre-walker.
- Nonslippery soles are a must!
- Try slipper socks, which come in various sizes, and are warm and flexible with a protective rubber sole. (They're also a lot harder to kick off than booties and socks.)

For the Walking, Talking Older Child...

Look around the store for styles and prices before you are waited on. Decide how much you want to spend and what type of shoes you want. Once the salesperson brings out the latest Snoopy or Smurf sneakers, it will be impossible to get your child to try on anything else!

Tell the salesperson what you want from the start, and you'll avoid unnecessary tears.

Shoe Tricks that Work

- Prevent falls by rubbing slippery new soles with sandpaper. Or press a strip of adhesive tape across each sole.
- The correct size (i.e., length) of shoelaces equals the number of holes multiplied by three.
- Rawhide shoelaces stay tied more easily if you soak them in warm water to soften them up.
- A strip of adhesive tape across the inside of the heel stops socks from creeping toward the toe of the shoe.
- Double-knot shoelaces to keep them from untying.
- Spray new sneakers with starch or fabric protector to keep dirt from becoming embedded.
- Put small plastic bags over shoes worn with boots, so the boots will slip off easily.
- Don't let children wear rubber or vinyl boots in school all day.
- And most important, *never use hand-me-down shoes!* No two children's feet are exactly the same size, so it's impossible to achieve a proper fit.

Sneakers

My children, at ages 6 and 9, don't feel comfortable wearing anything else. Because expensive shoes were cooling their heels in the back of the closet, I bought only sneakers for years. But certain occasions call for "real" shoes, now that the kids are older, and I'm back to buying both.

The theory that sneakers provide the same support for your child's feet as shoes is echoed by most pediatricians. But you might also consider the following information.

- Sneakers usually come in two widths, whereas shoes come in four to six widths.
- Shoes are getting more comfortable, because manufacturers have started making lighter, more flexible shoes for children.
- Unlike leather shoes, sneakers can cause moisture build-up, because the heat and dampness can't escape. Watch out for rashes, peeling skin, or other irritations caused by lack of ventilation (100 percent cotton socks will help absorb moisture).

CHAPTER 5

On the Go with Children

B.C. (Before Children), you put your coat on, got your keys, maybe checked to see that the coffee was turned off, and out you went. No muss, no fuss. A.D. (After Delivery) is a brand new ball game. Whether it's a walk to the park or a plane ride to Grandmom's house, every outing with Baby becomes an event. So get ready. You're about to become an expert on carriages, carriers, and travel planning.

The Travel Bag

Now when you go out, it's you, your child, and The Bag. Its contents may change over the years, but you will be forever carrying things for your children. (I may reach into my briefcase now and find a half-eaten box of raisins, an old apple core in a plastic bag, and some school notices!) Whether you're visiting friends or the doctor, going shopping, or on vacation, you will need to carry enough supplies to deal with a variety of situations and emergencies.

The Basic Bag I (Newborn to about 3 Years)

Fill it with the following minimum daily requirements:

- Disposable diapers (the number you need, plus one more)
- A roll of masking tape (in case the tape on the diaper won't stick)
- A small changing pad or blanket
- Extra pacifiers

- Extra bottle
- Premoistened towelettes
- A small pack of tissues
- Paper towels
- Plastic bags with ties (for neat disposal of snacks, diapers, etc.)
- Toys and books
- Change of clothing
- Band-Aids
- Folding umbrella

And Each Time You Go Out, Add...

- Fresh snacks
- Bottles filled with juice or water
- A damp washcloth in a tied plastic bag
- Additional clothing, weather demanding
- Any other supplies used up from the Basic Bag

The Basic Bag II (3 to 9 Years)

Although you don't *need* a special bag for this age group, it will add to the convenience of doing errands with your children if you carry the following items along:

- Collapsible cup (for short kids and tall drinking fountains)
- Something to drink (try a canteen filled with water or juice)
- Small pack of tissues
- Premoistened towelettes
- Plastic bags with ties
- A small pad and pen or Magic Marker
- Band-Aids
- Sugarless gum
- Extra sweater

Carriages, Strollers, and Baby Carriers

You can take even a newborn baby along when you're shopping, doing errands, visiting, or picking up older siblings at school, as long as you have the right set of wheels! Until your child becomes completely mobile and can keep up with your pace—usually at 3 or 4 years—you will need a *stroller*, *carrier*, or *carriage*. Transportation will change as your child grows.

When my children were small, they went through one carriage, five umbrella strollers, one baby carrier, and a bicycle seat for my husband's bike. If I'd known what I know now, I would have bought a different quality and combination of equipment and saved myself a lot of time, energy, and money. The following information should help you do just that.

Before You Buy, Consider...

- Your baby's head needs support until he gains control of his muscles (around 3 months).
- Carriages and infant strollers should have a complete reclining position so that the baby can lie flat on his back or stomach.
- Newborn to 6-month-old babies must be protected from intense heat, wind, and cold.
- Is your back strong enough to carry your baby in a carrier? If so, a carrier is fine for you.
- Do you most walk, drive, take a bus or subway? If you drive or take a subway or bus, you will need a lightweight, portable piece of equipment that folds.
- Do you spend a great deal of time outside the house, in parks, playgrounds, shopping malls, or visiting friends? If you're on the go a lot, you'll need equipment the baby can nap in, and where you can easily change and feed him.
- Are you or your husband tall? If so, the equipment you choose should have extension handles.
- Are there steps leading into your house or apartment building? My building had four small steps, but with a carriage or heavy stroller, the four steps felt like 400.
- Do you have limited space to store the equipment? If so, folding equipment is a must.

Carriages

Carriages are the most popular choice for these good reasons:

- Most carriages are designed for use from birth to 1 year, except for those that convert into strollers and can be used until age 4.
- They also provide the greatest protection against harsh winter

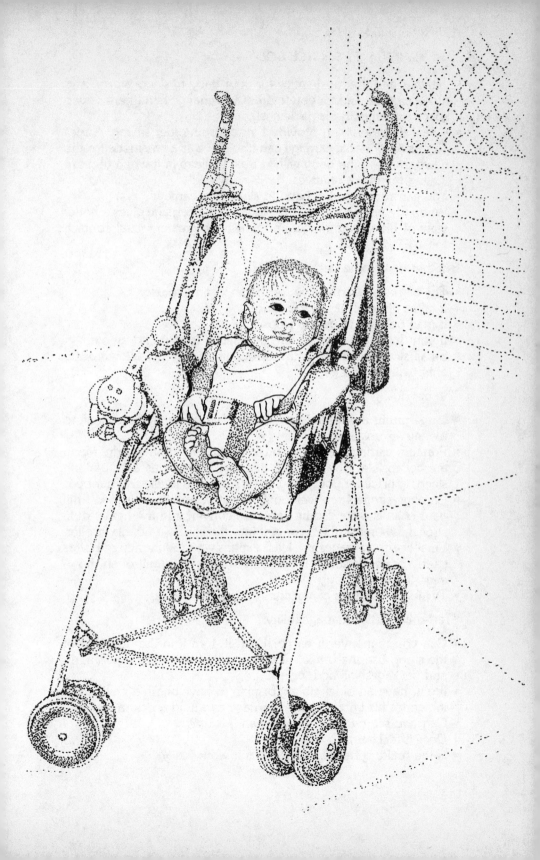

weather and the most space for your baby to sleep, sit up, and move around, and for you to dress and change him (there's even space underneath for packages!).

- A seat accessory can provide a ride for an older sibling. A medium-size, portable carriage can also serve as a bassinette for the newborn. And the baby will be able to sleep in it when you are visiting friends or relatives.
- You can rock a crying baby to sleep in a carriage.
- When the baby's awake, the height of the carriage gives a better view of his surroundings, and you have greater visual contact, too.

But there are some detractors:

- The carriage is expensive for the short time in use.
- It takes up a lot of storage space.
- It may be hard to get up steps.
- If you drive, the carriage can be difficult to fold and unfold.
- Small stores or stores with narrow aisles may not allow you to enter with a carriage.

The options:

- Large prams are durable and heavy, but they may be difficult to maneuver upstairs.
- Portable carriages are well-built, lightweight, and sturdy. Many are collapsible. The carriage bed can be used as a take-along sleeping place for your baby, but it's not safe to use as a car bed.
- Carriage-strollers are well-built, versatile, and can be used until your child is older. Some carriages convert into the heavy-duty stroller, whereas others convert into the sturdy umbrella stroller.
- Smaller-size carriages are least expensive, though they're not as sturdy or comfortable. If you don't plan on using it often, however, it is a good buy.
- Twin-size carriages can accommodate two babies.

"Test-drive" it for manageability:

- Can you maneuver it easily? Push it, turn it in the doorway of the store, use the brake. Remember that the baby, equipment, and packages will add weight.
- If you have an older sibling or plan to have another child close in age to this baby, check if carriage can hold an extra seat.
- Can you see over the hood when it is up?
- Does it feel sturdy?
- Is the brake system secure? Does it work easily?

- With portable or convertible carriages, see if it folds and unfolds smoothly. Make sure there's a feature that prevents accidental collapsing.
- Check for a suspension system that absorbs bumps.
- See that the interior is well padded.
- Look out for protruding parts or sharp edges.

Accessories

You'll need a new mattress and fitted sheet. For your newborn use a dry-down, soft waterproofing, and a cotton diaper over the sheet to save on extra laundry.

- A package rack is a great convenience.
- A carriage bag stores diapers, bottles, toys, your purse, and such.
- A rain or weather cover, if it's not built into the model you choose.
- Pram toys that fasten onto brackets on the hood will make traveling fun.
- For safety's sake, a harness is important.

Safety Tips for Carriages

- When you stop, always make sure that you've put on the brakes.
- When your baby is old enough to move around, use the harness to prevent him from toppling out.
- Even after you've bought your carriage, keep checking for protruding parts.
- Look out for small objects that may have fallen into the carriage.
- Never leave your child unattended in the carriage.

Strollers

Strollers are used from 6 months to 3 to 4 years. Some strollers are specifically made for newborns. Check the recommended age set by the manufacturer. They are probably the most convenient transportation for 6-month-olds to toddlers. However, they don't provide much protection from the elements.

If you plan on doing errands with your baby; if you take motorcycles and sand toys to the playground; if you plan to take the baby when walking your older child to school, try *two* strollers: one heavy-duty model for shopping and playground visits (When looking at carriages you might want to look at one that converts into a heavy-duty stroller.) and a folding umbrella stroller for car and bus trips.

If you drive a lot, you'll need a stroller only for short trips to the shopping mall; a single sturdy umbrella stroller will be enough.

Newborn strollers fold down so that the baby can lie flat on his back or stomach. A complete line of accessories is available, but it's sturdy and heavy to carry. These strollers don't give much protection from winter weather.

You may choose heavy-duty strollers, used from 3 months (or when baby can hold up head) to 3 to 4 years. They're even heavier and sturdier, but they can be taken on a bus. They are tough to carry up and down steps.

Sturdy umbrella strollers are designed for use from 3 months (or when baby can hold up head) to 3 to 4 years. They are lightweight and collapsible. You can collapse it in seconds while holding the baby in your other arm, hook it over your arm, and go up and down stairs or in or out of buses. These strollers are moderately priced. They are not as sturdy as heavy-duty strollers, however, and cannot be loaded with packages and playground toys.

A less-expensive umbrella stroller can be used from 3 months to 3 to 4 years. They're good only for short hops to Grandma's house, trips or vacations, but they are not built to withstand everyday use.

Double strollers are also designed for use from 3 months to 3 to 4 years. They're perfect for twins or siblings who are close in age. One type is made by attaching two sturdy umbrella strollers to each other (the strollers can be separated when necessary). Or you may choose a specially made heavy-duty stroller in which the seats are facing each other.

What to Look For in a Stroller

- It should be sturdy, easy to maneuver, simple to collapse and fold with one hand (if it's an umbrella stroller), and not too heavy for you to manage on stairs.
- The height of the handlebars should be comfortable for both you and your husband (some come with extension handles).
- Can it be adjusted to various positions—flat, semireclining, or upright?

- Does it have a secure restraining system with a harness and crotch belt?
- Are the brakes secure?
- Does it provide a way of carrying packages?
- Is there a footrest?
- Are there accessories to fit the stroller?

Accessories

- Rain cover
- Weather cover or hood
- Carrying bag
- Extension handles for the taller parent
- Footrest
- Umbrella
- Wind shield
- Boot sack (a warm blanket shaped like a sleeping bag)
- Package rack (for heavy-duty strollers)

Safety Tips for Strollers

- Travel light—the stroller will tip over if you put too much weight in the handlebar bag.
- Make sure your child's feet are on the footrest, so they don't drag on the ground.
- Always use the safety belt.
- Check that the brakes are on when you stop.

Baby Carriers

A great way of transporting baby whenever a carriage or stroller is too much—such as shopping in a crowded store, going on escalators, visiting museums with "no stroller" rules, walking in the woods. And you'll enjoy the extra cuddling the carrier design affords. It's an expensive piece of equipment, so think carefully about how much you'll use it.

It is important to practice "loading" and "unloading" your baby, until you can do it quickly and comfortably.

Some Options for Baby Carriers

- The front infant carrier can be used for newborn to 3 to 4 months (see manufacturer's recommendations). It should have a head support and be made of soft material.
- The back carrier with frame is designed for use from 7 months (or when baby can sit up by himself) until 1½ years (or until he gets too heavy for you to carry comfortably).
- The bicycle seat is only for babies who can sit up firmly (around 7 months) and can be used up to 4 years (or until your child reaches the manufacturer's recommended weight). Riding with a young child can be a fun, free, and easy way of getting around. Just make sure your child always wears a helmet.

What to Look For in a Bicycle Seat

- Good heel and leg protection
- A secure seat belt
- Sturdy footrests (to protect little feet from getting caught in the spokes of the rear wheel).

Traveling by Car

Car Seats Are Essential

Your newborn should use a car seat from the very first time he or she rides in the car, no matter how short the ride. Holding a baby in your arms in a car, or fastening an adult seat belt around you and the baby can cause the child severe internal injuries in a crash. Over 2,000 babies and children under the age of 4 are killed in car accidents each year. Let your child learn from the start that using a restraining system in the car is the natural way to travel.

When the child reaches age 5 (or 40 pounds) be sure she always sits in the back seat and uses the car seat belt.

Car Seat Options

Car seats should be constructed with molded seat, metal frames, some form of padding and harness system. Infants require a reclining sitting position in a car seat because developmentally their muscles have not matured to the point where they can sit up.

- *The Infant Car Seat* is designed to be used until the baby is approximately 18 pounds (9 to 15 months). It has one reclining position. As the baby grows, you will have to purchase a car seat that has adjustable sitting positions to meet the weight and height of the growing child.
- *The Car Seat with Adjustable Positions* is designed to be used for a newborn through age 3 years or older, depending on the manufacturer's age recommendation for use.
- *The Child Seat* is designed for the 3- to 5-year-old. This seat, while providing a safe restraining system, allows the child to have greater freedom of movement and view. This is important for this age group.

What to Look For in a Car Seat

- Choose a car seat with a seal from the National Highway and Traffic Safety Administration stating that it has met the mandatory requirements set by the Federal government. If you can't find a car seat with a seal of approval, contact the:

  National Highway & Traffic Safety Administration
  400 Seventh Street, S.W.
  Washington, D.C. 20590
  (202) 426-2264

Another resource is a small booklet "Don't Risk Your Child's Life," published by Physicians for Automotive Safety. This guide has recent information on car restraining systems including a list of safe crash-tested devices, brand names and model numbers. To receive this booklet just send $.35 plus a stamped 4¾" by 11" self-addressed envelope to:

  Physicians for Automotive Safety
  P.O. Box 208
  Rye, N.Y. 10580

- Select a car seat that is easy to install and remove from your car. Try the model out in your car to see if it fits the car's seating area and restraining system. A poorly anchored car seat acts as a launching pad in a crash.
- The seat should be a comfortable place for your child to sit and sleep. Look for car seats that have reclining positions and side panels

your child can rest her head against when napping so the head doesn't bob around. Also check for elevated seats that allow the child to see out the windows.

Surviving Long Trips

Traveling for more than ½ hour in a car can be hard on young children. I remember each time we got into the car, my 3-year-old would ask, "Are we almost there?"

To protect your car from permanent damage, put a sheet over the backseat to catch crumbs and spills. A shoe bag over the back of the front seat to store toys, snacks, and cleaning supplies will add to your peace of mind. Choose a few of the following items to fill the bag. (They will come in handy on any day-long outing, too.)

- Toys and books
- Tape recorder and tapes (children's stories or songs)
- Paper and crayons (use a long cake pan for the children to color in)
- Wrap inexpensive books or toys in gift paper and save for the low points of the trip
- Thermos filled with cold water; paper cups
- Juice (Avoid grape juice. It will stain if it spills.)
- Snacks (The best choices are foods that are not sticky and don't leave crumbs.)
- Paper towels
- Plastic bags with ties for garbage
- Premoistened towels or wet washcloth stored in plastic bag for cleaning hands and faces
- Tissues
- Pillow
- *When traveling with young child, bring your basic bag filled with the recommended supplies.*

If the trip is over 1 hour, plan to make stops to stretch. Call the Chamber of Commerce in a few towns you will be passing through and inquire about playgrounds or places of interest for children. It's fun to combine traveling and visiting. It breaks up the monotony of the trip. Even a McDonald's with a playground can be a lifesaver.

Traveling by Plane or Train

Inquire ahead about special services for parents with young children. Many airports or train stations have personnel to help you aboard with your children and luggage. Some terminals even set aside a special space for mothers to change and nurse their babies. Find out what equipment you can carry on the plane or train (stroller, infant seat, car seat, etc.). Try to get the bulkhead seat on the plane. It is the most spacious area and will enable a young child to stand up and move around without bothering the person in the seat in front.

Planning Day Outings with Your Kids

- Always verify information you've been given about the place you plan to visit.
- Inquire about age-appropriate activities at facility. One time we went to an amusement park that had no rides for children under 6 years.
- Ask if strollers are allowed.
- Ask if refreshment stands are available and picnics allowed.
- Call the local Chamber of Commerce of the town you plan to visit. Ask about:

> Other places of interest or special events nearby
> Picnic areas
> Playgrounds
> Swimming with changing facilities
> McDonald's or Burger King

Planning Family Vacations with Young Children

- State Departments of Tourism, Vacation Bureau, or Travel usually have lots of literature available to you in planning your vacation.

Write to the specific states you might be interested in visiting and explain your interests and ages of your children. You will probably receive some interesting material to sift through.

Once you have narrowed down your selection, explore the following:

- Is the space safe for young children or will you have to monitor every movement your child takes?
- Is the facility, neighborhood, or community geared to families with young children? It is very helpful to have children around that your children can play with.
- What are the recreational facilities like for children? Are they age-appropriate for your children? One year we rented a house in a recreational community. The brochure stated swimming for the family. However, they had no shallow water under 4 inches or a kiddie pool.
- Are baby-sitters available?
- Are there informal, family-style restaurants nearby?

CHAPTER 6

Growing Up Healthy and Safe

Parents are the overall managers of the health and well-being of their children. As consumers, we select pediatricians, dentists, first aid and general medical supplies. We child-proof our living space, teach personal safety, and help stimulate the physical, social, and intellectual development of our little ones. The following section will cover all the important facts you need to know about helping your child grow up healthy and safe.

Medical Care

Finding a Good Pediatrician

Your *pediatrician*, a doctor who specializes in treating children, can be a great source of information and reassurance. A good pediatrician has a lot of patience (with parents as well as children!), and sense of humor and, of course, excellent medical skills. You should start looking for a pediatrician about a month before your baby is due. Ask for referrals from friends who have children, or from your obstetrician, midwife, or childbirth instructor. Or you can call the pediatrics department of your local hospital for names of staff pediatricians in private practice.

Once you have a list, arrange to meet with each of the doctors before your baby is born. And when you do, the following questions should help you make your choice.

What Are the Doctor's Qualifications?

Is he/she...

- Board certified as a specialist in pediatric medicine?
- A member of professional organizations?
- On the medical or teaching staff of a local hospital? (Hospital affiliations make admissions and referrals much easier.)

How Do You Get Along with the Doctor?

- Do you feel comfortable with him/her?
- Does the doctor seem receptive to questions? Compassionate? Concerned?

How Is the Practice Organized?

- Is the office easy to get to in all kinds of weather? (During the first year, you'll need to visit the pediatrician just about every month for well-baby checkups.)
- If you work, does the doctor have weekend, evening, or early morning office hours?
- What's the average length of time you'll have to sit in the waiting room?
- Does the doctor make house calls?
- Does he/she have a regular "telephone hour"?
- Can most simple tests be done in the office, or are they sent to labs that cost more time and money?
- What is the doctor's fee schedule?
- Is it a group or solo practice? How many doctors "cover" for yours when he/she is unavailable?
- Is there a 24-hour answering service?
- Does the doctor allow at least 15 minutes for a routine checkup?
- Is there enough time during each appointment to ask questions without feeling rushed?

When in Doubt...

...you can always change doctors. Just go back to your original list and try again with another pediatrician, now that you know what you do and don't want in a physician for your child.

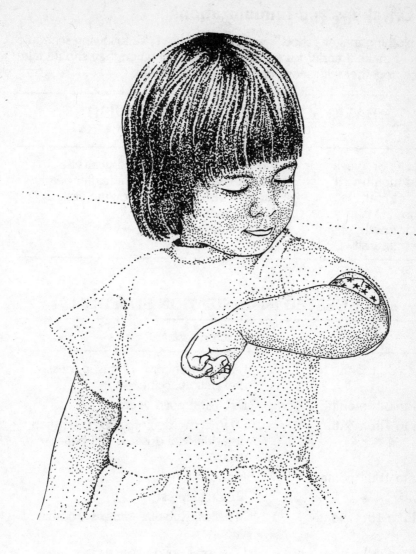

Keeping in Touch with Your Pediatrician

It's easy when you keep all your questions jotted down in a small notebook to bring to office visits or refer to on the phone. Keep your pharmacist's number in here, too, so it's handy when the doctor wants to call in a prescription.

Checkups and Immunizations

Nothing makes "shots" easy for kids—but the following schedule should make it easier for you to keep track of when they should take place, together with those regular well-baby visits:

BASIC SCHEDULE OF ROUTINE VISITS TO THE PEDIATRICIAN

- 2d to 3d week visit
- 2d month visit
- 4th to 5th month visit
- 6th to 7th month visit

- 9th to 10th month visit
- 1st-year visit
- 15th-month visit
- 18th-month visit

- 2d-year visit
- thereafter yearly routine visits

SUGGESTED IMMUNIZATION SCHEDULE

Age	Vaccine/Tests
2d to 3d month	DTP (diphtheria, tetanus, pertussis), oral polio vaccine
4th to 5th month	DTP, oral polio vaccine
6th to 7th month	DTP (some doctors also recommend an additional dose of oral polio vaccine)
9th to 10th month	Blood test
1 year	Tuberculin test
12th to 15th month	Measles, Rubella, Mumps (combined vaccine)
18th month	DTP, oral polio vaccine
2d year	Tuberculin test
4–6 year	DTP booster, polio booster
14–16 year	TD (tetanus-diphtheria toxoid adult type)*

---

*Tetanus-Diphtheria (TD) booster every 10 years or after a contaminated wound if it has been more than 5 years since the previous tetanus shot.

Immunization Record

To stay on schedule, you'll need to keep a written record of your child's immunizations and boosters, so that you'll know when each series is complete, and when boosters are due. Then you'll have the record ready to present when your child starts school, goes to camp, or if you move and change doctors. You can get a record like this from your pediatrician or health department. Take it with you whenever you visit the doctor. Also keep a list of your child's major illnesses and the dates when they occurred.

Name_____ Sex_____ Birthdate_____			
Vaccine	Date Given	Doctor or Clinic	Date Next Dose Due
Polio (Recommended at about 2 months of age)			
DTP (diphtheria, tetanus, pertussis) DT (for infants who are allergic to pertussis vaccine) TD (for age 6 years and older)			
Measles, Rubella, Mumps Recommended at age 15 months. Given singly or in a combination dose. TB test (at about 1 year)			
Other tests or vaccines given			

The Well-Stocked Medicine Chest

I remember one harrowing evening when Marc had a high fever, and I called our pediatrician, who suggested a common over-the-counter drug. We didn't have any, though, and I had to call every pharmacy in the Yellow Pages before I found one that was still open. From then on, I've kept a well-stocked medicine cabinet, *and* a backup list of drugstores that are open on weekends and evenings. (It's also a good idea to find out which ones deliver, because it's hard to get out of the house with a sick child.)

Here's a list of over-the-counter drugs and first-aid supplies you'll probably want on hand—but don't forget: *Always check with your pediatrician before giving drugs to small children.*

Nonprescription Drugs and Supplies to Keep in Stock

- Antidiarrhea agent (Kaopectate)
- Antiseptic cleanser (hydrogen peroxide or Betadine)
- Antiseptic cream to apply on minor cuts or burns
- Auralgan (temporary relief from ear irritation)
- Baby aspirin
- Cotton balls
- Calamine lotion (for bites)
- Cough syrup
- Decongestant
- Ice pack
- Rubbing alcohol
- Ipecac syrup (to induce vomiting in case of accidental poisoning)
- Ointment for rashes
- Tigan suppository (when child can't take aspirin because of vomiting)
- 2 *rectal* thermometers
- Petroleum jelly
- Measured medicine cup (Great! Put the medicine in a small measured cup and the child drinks it up. No more spills from child pushing the teaspoon away.)
- Humidifier or vaporizer

Your pediatrician may prefer other specific brand-name products. Be sure to ask. Also, every six months check the labels of drugs you have in stock. Note the expiration date and throw out any that are past their prime.

Vitamins

Most pediatricians recommend a liquid vitamin supplement during the baby's first year. If you and your pediatrician decide to continue the vitamin supplement as your child gets older, you will probably switch to chewable vitamins. Children like the flavored ones shaped like T.V. characters. However, you must impress upon your child that vitamins are not candy or special treats but should only be taken when given by mommy or daddy. They should be stored in the medicine cabinet with all the other medicines, OUT OF THE REACH OF CHIL-DREN.

Dental Care

Little Teeth Can Have Big Problems!

You probably know how to keep your own teeth healthy and sparkling, but believe me, children's dental needs are different. I learned this the hard way, letting my first child go to sleep with a bottle of milk or apple juice—never realizing that the sweet liquid would cause four severely decayed front teeth by the time Marc was 2½. But dental disasters like ours can be avoided.

Healthy Teeth—the Basics

- Talk to your dentist soon after your baby is born. He or she can answer any questions you may have and offer advice and suggestions.
- Cavities can form even in primary ("baby") teeth. To help prevent them, limit foods containing sugar, and clean your baby's teeth daily, wiping them with a piece of gauze or a washcloth.
- At age 1, you can start using a toothbrush. Brush your child's teeth mornings, evenings, and after meals—with nonfluoride toothpaste for children under age 4, who tend to swallow more than they spit out.
- When your child is around 3½, she's ready to solo, under supervision. An egg timer is a fun visual aid to show her how long to keep brushing. (The noise and novelty of an electric toothbrush may "turn on" the reluctant brusher!)

Finding a Good Dentist

- Age 2 is a good time for the first visit, which should include meeting the dentist and getting a look at "the chair" and other equipment. (Before you go, ask what the dentist plans to do, so you can prepare your child.)

- If you're thinking of using your own dentist, consider whether you think he or she and your child would be comfortable with each other.
- If your child is often fearful or shy, you may want to consult a *pedodontist*—a dentist who's had two years of special training in children's dentistry. A pedodontist's staff, office, and equipment are all geared to young children. For a referral, ask your own dentist or pediatrician, or call a local dental school.
- Then keep up all this good work by scheduling a checkup every six months. Make a note on your calendar a month early, to make sure you get an appointment.

Developmental Highlights

It helps to have a general understanding of the developmental phases that most children go through. Each child has his or her own timetable, though. That means that your child's behavior might not coincide exactly with the so-called average.

By the time your child is 5, it won't really matter when he learned to walk, run, and climb, talk, brush his teeth, use the toilet, drink from cups, and so on. What will matter is simply that he can do the things that most healthy children his age can do. During routine visits to the pediatrician, discuss any questions you might have concerning your child's development.

There are several reassuring guides to children's developmental stages. A few of the best are:

- *The First Three Years of Life* by Burton L. White (Avon, 1984).
- *The Psychological Birth of the Human Infant* by Margaret S. Mahler et al. (Basic Books, 1975).

The following chart is based on the developmental highlights discussed in those books.

BIRTH to 6 MONTHS

Common Behavior	Average Age
Main concern is to achieve physical comfort (to be fed, dry, held, soothed, etc.)	Birth to 4 weeks

BIRTH to 6 MONTHS (*cont.*)

Common Behavior	Average Age
Does not understand how he is comforted	Birth to 4 weeks
Focuses on the eyes of person holding him	Birth to 6 weeks
Oriented toward the world within a yard or so of him	Birth to 5½ months
Begins to strike at objects within reach	6 weeks to 3½ months
No longer content just to look at an object. He wants to get his hand into his exploration efforts. The world must be brought near to him to explore	6 weeks to 3½ months
Listens to his own sounds	6 weeks to 3½ months
Able to focus clearly at distances between 6 and 12 inches	6 weeks
Develops a store of memories of pleasurable and painful feelings based on mothering experiences to relieve physical discomfort	2 to 3 months
First social smile (any face). Strong interest in human faces	2 to 3 months
Will socialize with anyone	2 to 3 months
Looks at objects and brings to mouth to be gummed	2 to 3 months
Turning eyes and body to the source of the sound	3½ to 5½ months

BIRTH to 6 MONTHS (*cont.*)

Common Behavior	Average Age
Holding head in an upright position when lying on stomach	4 months
Begins to know mother. Can differentiate mother by her smell, her touch, and sight	4 to 5 months
Perceptually explores his environment	4 to 5 months
Develops confidence in parenting. Expects to be cared for	4 to 5 months
Can identify the mother's voice	4 to 5 months
Sits with assistance	4 to 6 months
Turning or rolling over	4 to 6 months
Directed visual reaching	4 to 8 months
Develops action pattern of holding objects or clasps objects with both hands and transferring object from hand to hand	3 to 3½ months
Can hold bottle with support	3 to 3½ months
Hearing approaches that of a normal adult	3½ months
Begins to form a special relationship with mother or major caretaker	3½ months
Hearty laughter and responds to tickling and playfulness	3½ months
Starts to gurgle and make delightful sounds	3½ months

BIRTH to 6 MONTHS (*cont.*)

Common Behavior	Average Age
Can adjust the focus of eyes from object at all distances and has near mature visual ability to keep both eyes on an object	3½ months
Seems to enjoy the presence of other people	3½ to 5½ months
Awake at least half of waking hours and enjoys playing	3½ to 5½ months
Visual and reaching explorations	3½ to 5½ months
Head control when in a sitting position	3 months
Firmly holds head unsupported	3 to 4 months
Socializes solely with primary caretakers	3 to 6 months
Gathers information through visual exploration	3 to 9 months
Great visual interest combined with hand-eye activities (looking, touching and gumming)	3 to 9 months
Interested in own sounds and listens to words	3 to 9 months
Enjoys watching other children	5 to 7 months
Responds to sounds. Does not understand the meaning of any words but rather the familiarity with the qualities of the voices	5 to 8 months
Sitting up unassisted	5 to 8 months

BIRTH to 6 MONTHS (*cont.*)

Common Behavior	Average Age
Enjoys playing with small objects that he can hold (not too small that he might choke)	5 to 8 months
Visual interest in fine small particles (crumbs, specks, etc.)	5 to 8 months
Interested in action on objects (dropping, throwing, opening things, banging)	5 to 8 months
First tooth	5 to 12 months
Interested in parts of their body (hands and feet) and the relationship of the parts	5½ months
Within the nuclear family likes to play social games, sing, talk, laugh together	5 to 7 months
Abrupt mood changes (crying to laughing)	5½ to 8 months
Baby accepts abuses of older siblings	Birth to 8 months

6 MONTHS to 12 MONTHS

Common Behavior	Average Age
Maneuvers to a sitting position	6 to 9 months
Crawling (scooting)	6 months to 1 year

6 MONTHS to 12 MONTHS (*cont.*)

Common Behavior	Average Age
Extreme orientation toward the primary caretaker which in most instances is the mother	6 months to 2 years
Stranger anxiety. Preference and comfort with nuclear family. Shy or apprehensive with people outside the family	7 to 11 months
Pulls self up on furniture	7 to 14 months
Climbing 6 inches (including stairs)	7 to 17 months
Children learn to understand language earlier and at a more rapid rate than they learn to use it orally. First words understood	8 months to 1 year
Begins to understand concept of cause and effect. (Child begins to turn things on and off, in and out, opening and closing, filling and emptying, standing objects up, pushing objects, etc.)	8 to 15 months
Makes gestures of affection for primary caretakers	8 to 14 months
Period of curiosity	8 to 14 months
Love of physical exploration	8 to 14 months
Interested in mastering the use of his body	8 to 14 months
Practices new motor skills until successful	8 to 14 months
Joy in exploring and learning	8 to 14 months

6 MONTHS to 12 MONTHS (*cont.*)

Common Behavior	Average Age
Enjoys and loves practicing his ability to move through space in all directions	8 to 14 months
First words understood	8 months to 1 year

Mommy	Shoe
Daddy	Ball
Names of family	Cookie
members	Juice
and pets	No-no
Bye-bye	Wave bye-bye
Baby	

Common Behavior	Average Age
Climbing 12 inches	8 to 15 months
Peak of curiosity	8 to 15 months
Explores how body goes. Busy practicing crawling, climbing, cruising and walking	8 to 15 months
Explores in detail qualities of small objects	8 to 15 months
Stands with support	8 to 15 months
Staring behavior (gains information through vision)	8 months to 15 months
Walking while holding on to a support	9 to 15 months
Walking unassisted	9 to 18 months
First simple instructions understood	9 months to 2 years
Stands alone	10 to 15 months
Climbing downstairs	10 to 15 months

6 MONTHS to 12 MONTHS (*cont.*)

Common Behavior	Average Age
Begins to make clear request for assistance from caretaker	11 to 12 months
Begins to object to abuses of older siblings, especially with aggressive behavior and turns to adults for help	Begins 11 months

SECOND YEAR

Common Behavior			Average Age
General words understood			12 to 14 months
Hi	Come here	Socks	
Kitty (cat)	Sit down	Dance	
Dog (doggy)	Stand up	Patty-cake	
Cup	Get up	Peekaboo	
Cracker	Stop that	Kiss	
Car	Hug	Bring	
Eyes	Water	Give mommy	
Ears	Drink	Throw the ball	
Feet	Chair (high chair)	Brush your hair	
Hair	Book	Kiss me	
Knows something about his parents' disciplinary style			13 months
Baby begins to use tactics to get back at older siblings, so you will no longer be able to assume that all difficulties are initiated by the older child			13 months and up
Riding wheel toys without pedals			14 months

SECOND YEAR (*cont.*)

Common Behavior	Average Age
General words understood	14 to 18 months

Milk	Brush your hair
Spoon	(teeth)
Telephone (phone)	Where is
Keys	Turn on...
Blanket	Turn off the...
Bed	Open the door
Cereal	Close the door
Bottle	Go get...
Horse	Let's go...
Hat	Find
Coat (jacket, sweater)	Do you want
Apple	Don't touch
Teeth	Show me

Opposes will of primary caretaker (negativism)	14 to 24 months
Hanging around behavior. Seems somewhat purposeless	14 to 24 months
Able to hold real conversations	14 to 24 months
Usually spends relatively little time in his own room with toys	14 to 24 months
Personalities begin to become more defined. There is a clearer expression of individual traits of child	14 to 24 months
Turn pages of cardboard children's books	14 to 24 months
Basic control of the body	15 to 21 months
Running	20 months
Thinking before acting (manipulation of ideas in advance of motor action)	22 to 36 months

24 to 36 MONTHS

Common Behavior	Average Age
Uses objects for imaginative play	Around the second year
Interest in gymnastics	24 months
Interested in other children and interacting. Still likes solitary and parallel types of play	24 to 36 months
Lessening in intensity of the exclusive focus on the nuclear family and on mother	24 to 36 months
Asserting self and testing wills	24 to 36 months
Learning skills of leading and following in group situations	24 to 36 months
Increase in capacity to control impulses	24 to 36 months
Engages in fantasy activities (make believe)	24 to 36 months
Riding tricycle	24 to 36 months
Explores object and practices simple skills on objects, but combines these with social interaction with other children	24 to 36 months
Interested in language	24 to 36 months
Begins to develop interest in social relationships with friends	24 to 36 months
Creative activities	24 to 36 months
Working problems out by thinking them through	24 to 36 months

24 MONTHS to 36 MONTHS (*cont.*)

Common Behavior	Average Age
Egocentric thinker (sees things exclusively from own point of view)	24 to 36 months
Thought process (anything that moves is alive and accidental occurrence is difficult to understand)	24 to 36 months

THIRD YEAR

Common Behavior	Average Age
Beginning to sleep through the night without wetting bed	3 years
Walks up and down stairs alone	3 years
Likes to use crayons	3 years
Intense drive for perceptual clarification (constant questioning)	3 years
Words become instruments for expressing concepts, ideas, and relationships	3 years
Learns to clarify ideas and concepts through dramatic play	3 years
Learns to listen and listens to learn	3 years
Begins to understand the concept of bargaining	3 years
Desire to please	3 years

THIRD YEAR (*cont.*)

Common Behavior	Average Age
Can bargain	3 years
Beginning to express willingness to wait, share toys	3 years
Feeds self	3 years
Can pour from a pitcher	3 years
Interested in imitating and conforming	3 years
Greater interest and ability in dressing and undressing self	3 years
Gets over tantrums more quickly and when resisting he uses language rather than primitive methods of pushing, biting, scratching	3 years
Asks questions because appears to have a hunger for information	3 years

FOURTH YEAR

Common Behavior	Average Age
Laces his shoes	4 years
Buttons his clothes	4 years
Questions are directed to conceptualize, generalize and order his experiences	4 years
Little understanding of past and future	4 years

FOURTH YEAR (*cont.*)

Common Behavior	Average Age
Doesn't like to repeat things	4 years
Can carry on long and involved conversations	4 years
Combs his own hair with some supervision	4 years
Brushes his own teeth	4 years
Prefers groups of 2 or 3 children for play	4 years
Can be bossy in directing others	4 years
Talkative	4 years
Growing reasoning powers	4 years
Prone to unreasonable fears (e.g. the dark)	4 years
Unable to make realistic distinctions between truth and fable	4 years

FIFTH YEAR

Common Behavior	Average Age
Enjoys separation from home	5 years
Can brush hair, teeth, and wash face with little supervision	5 years

FIFTH YEAR (*cont.*)

Common Behavior	Average Age
Can put toys away in an orderly manner	5 years
Likes to finish what he has started	5 years
Can carry a plot in a story and can repeat a long sequence accurately	5 years
Can carry over a play project from 1 day to another	5 years
Paints with a plan	5 years
Ready and eager to know realities	5 years
Questions are fewer but more meaningful	5 years
Interested in the practical mechanisms of his world	5 years
Pragmatist (sees things in terms of use)	5 years
Fairy-tales with excessive unrealities are confusing	5 years
Dramatic play relates to everyday functions. Effort to express ideas and capture relationships through words rather than to indulge in make-believe	5 years
Egocentric-unaware of his own thinking as a subjective process separate from the objective world	5 years
Likes to make an impression on his friends	5 years

FIFTH YEAR (*cont.*)

Common Behavior	Average Age
Feels pride in accomplishments	5 years
Relatively independent and self-sufficient	5 years
Enjoys friendships and group activities	5 years

Home Safety

As soon as you catch your breath after the baby is born, begin to think about childproofing your home. Babies have no judgment in regard to safety. They are so eager to explore their world that they will do everything from sticking paper clips into electrical sockets to eating your favorite plant. So by the fifth month, your home should be completely childproofed.

Studies have shown that parents who try to anticipate accidents before they happen prevent many mishaps. Most parents try their best to supervise their child's play, but because babies move fast, keeping an eye on them is not enough. Even the best of us are distracted sometimes, and that's just when an accident is most likely to happen. By making our homes as safe as possible, we have an extra measure of safety for the times when we can't give children 100 percent of our attention.

Once, a large bookcase fell on my younger child. We both were in the same room. I had emptied out a 6-foot-high bookcase that I was planning to dust and wax. The phone rang. I turned around to answer it... and only seconds later I heard a crash and a shriek. Fortunately, Marc was not seriously hurt. The next day I had a workman bolt the bookcase to the wall.

Childproofing goes beyond rearranging your home to meet certain safety standards. You will also have to change certain habits: refrain from absentmindedly leaving coffee cups on the table; the toilet lid up; earrings on your bureau; and handbags, razors, cigarette lighters, and so forth in easily accessible places, not just for your child's protection, but for yours.

I have lost two sets of keys and one watch by the quick hands of my little toddler. I know they are in the house somewhere but it has been three years since they were last seen, and my pediatrician assured me Marc couldn't have swallowed them.

Although childproofing does change your living space, it is well worth the trouble and inconvenience to insure the safety of your child. *Remember, this stage doesn't last forever.*

Protective Equipment

- Automatic smoke alarm.
- Baby bumpers on furniture to turn sharp corners into soft corners.
- Cabinet locks and/or safety latches for cabinets and drawers.
- Doorknob stoppers that prevent children from turning knobs.
- Drawer stoppers to keep drawers from being pulled out completely.
- Guards and stops for windows, to prevent windows from being opened beyond a certain height.
- Refrigerator safety catch.
- Top-of-door lock.
- Shock stops for electrical sockets or plastic plugs for electrical outlets. Watch out, though. An agile toddler with interest might be able to pull the stops out.
- Safety gates for stairs and doors.

How to Childproof Your Home

- Cover all electrical outlets with plastic plugs, lock-it devices, or outlets covers.
- Equip windows with window guards or stops. Don't put furniture or any other possible "stepping stool" near windows. (In some cities, landlords are responsible for putting guards on apartment-house windows.)
- Stairs should have security gates. Block in the spindles if they're wide enough to let your child crawl through.
- Old paint—manufactured prior to February 1978—may contain high levels of lead, which can cause brain damage if eaten by small children. Check any wall in your home for peeling lead-based paint or plaster.
- Cover sharp or pointed furniture edges with bumpers, or remove them until your child is older. Glass tables, at this stage, are an accident waiting to happen.

- Put stoppers on drawers to prevent curious children from pulling the drawer out.
- Bolt bookcases, breakfronts, and other easily toppled pieces of furniture to the wall.
- Make sure that you have an extra set of keys, for doors that can be locked from the outside. Or you can take out the lock, or install doorknob stoppers.
- To keep fragile objects in one piece, make sure they're out of reach.
- Place rubber mats under scatter rugs to prevent slipping.
- Bells on your doors make a cheerful sound to let you know when a little adventurer leaves the house.
- If you have glass doors, place a piece of colored tape on the glass at the child's eye level.
- When your baby is in the crib, playpen, swing, or high chair, be sure there's nothing dangerous within reach.
- If you have a piano, a strip of cork at each end of the keyboard cover will protect your young child's fingers.
- Heaters, fireplaces, and wood stoves should be surrounded with safety barriers.
- Install smoke alarms and periodically check batteries.
- Check all closets for mothballs or deodorizers. If you use mothballs in the closet, lock the closet doors.
- Tie up all drape and venetian blind cords.
- Check for small objects that may have fallen on the floor, and might trip up toddlers.
- Turn your water heater down to 120° to 130° so that water never gets too hot for little hands.
- Tape extension cords to the wall or under pieces of furniture.
- See Fireproofing Techniques on page 50.

Most of us would not think about our household plants or flowers from our garden as potentially dangerous. However, some are poisonous if sampled by curious little ones and should be placed out of a young child's reach. Check the following list for common poisonous plants.

COMMON POISONOUS PLANTS

Common Name	Botanical Name
Azalea	Rhododendron*
Black Nightshade	Solanum
Buttercup	Ranunculus
Caladium	Caladium* (poison-irritant)**
Castor Oil Plant	Ricinus communis
Christmas Pepper	Capsicum annum (poison-irritant)
Daffodil	Narcissus pseudonarcissus
Deadly Nightshade	Atropa belladonna
Dumbcane	Dieffenbachia* (poison-irritant)
English Ivy	Hedera helix
Foxglove	Digitalis purpurea
Fruit Pits	Prunus*
Holly	Llex*
Hyacinth	Hyacinthus orientalis
Hydrangea	Hydrangea arborescens
Iris	Iris*
Jack-in-the-Pulpit	Arisaema triphyllum (poison-irritant)
Jerusalem Cherry	Solanum pseudocapsicum
Jimson Weed	Datura stramonium
Lily-of-the-Valley	Convallaria majalis
Mayapple	Podophyllum peltatum
Mistletoe	Phoradendron flavescens
Mountain Laurel	Kalmia latifolia
Nephthytis	Nephthytis* (poison-irritant)
Philodendron	Philodendron* (poison-irritant)
Pokeweed	Phytolacca americana
Pothos	Scindapsus aureus (poison-irritant)
Privet	Ligustrum vulgare
Rhododendron	Rhododendron maximum
Tomato Plant	Lycopersicon esculentum
Yew	Taxus*

* Includes all species of the plant.

**Poison/irritant: Plants whose primary effect is burns or irritation to the mouth or throat and which may have other harmful effects.

Note: *This list does not include every poisonous plant. Remember to report all plant ingestions to local Poison Control Center.*

Bathroom

- Store all drugs in a *locked* cabinet.
- Keep the toilet lid down when the toilet is not in use.
- Don't buy any medicine that doesn't come with childproof cap.
- Mark hot water faucet with a strip of bright red tape.
- Check the expiration date on all medicines before using.
- Place a mat or nonslip strips on the bottom of the bathtub.
- If you use a toilet deodorizer, make sure it's the kind that goes *into* the tank, not the type that hangs over the rim of the bowl.

Kitchen/Dining Room

- Store all chemicals (detergents, cleaning fluids, bleach, insecticide, etc.) in a locked cabinet.
- Fold tablecloth edges up on top of table and out of a toddler's curious reach.
- Keep sharp knives and scissors in a separate safe place.
- Remove burner knobs when you're not using the stove.
- Use the *back* burners whenever you can. If you must use the front burners, turn pot handles toward the back of the stove.
- Don't let appliance cords dangle temptingly over the edge of a counter or table. Always unplug appliances when not in use.
- Lock any cabinets that contain dishes, glasses, or other fine breakables.
- Don't leave the cup from the dishwasher out. An inquisitive baby may scoop out and eat the detergent.
- Utility ladders and stools can pose a hazardous mountain-climbing challenge, so don't leave them alone with little ones.
- Garbage can be alluring—to very young children, at least. So keep your trash can under the sink and lock cabinet door if possible.

Child's Room

- Curtains, rugs, and linens should be flameproof.
- Remove dangerous objects that can be reached from a crib.
- For super safety tips on second-hand or hand-me-down equipment, furniture and toys: check Consumer Product Safety Commission Hotline 1-800-638-2772. They can tell you which models

of dangerous toys and equipment have been recalled by manufacturers. Know name, serial number, and manufacturer before
calling.

Outside

- Keep outside play equipment away from fences and walls.
- Install swings, climbing equipment, and so forth over a "cush-
ioned" surface such as sand or sawdust.
- Banish any poisonous plants or flowers (see page 101 for list).
- Watch out for water hazards. If you've a lily pond, fill it in until
your children are old enough to appreciate it without falling in.
Swimming pools should be fenced, plastic pools should be emp-
tied when not in use.

Garage, Hobby, or Laundry Areas

Poisons and sharp or heavy tools belong in locked cabinets or on
high shelves.

In Others' Homes

- Watch your child carefully in non-childproofed homes.
- When friends or relatives baby-sit (in their homes or yours), you'll
all feel safer if you inform them of the safety precautions you
usually take for your child.

Emergency telephone numbers should be posted at all times:

EMERGENCY TELEPHONE NUMBERS

Mother's Work Number   _____

Father's Work Number   _____

Doctor: _____

    Address   _____

    Phone   _____

EMERGENCY TELEPHONE NUMBERS (*cont.*)

Hospital: _____

    Address   _____

    Phone   _____

Fire Department   _____

Ambulance   _____

Police   _____

    Local Precinct   _____

Friends   _____

Relatives   _____

Local Poison Control Center   _____

Drugstore   _____

Where you can be reached (tape a card with place, address, and phone number).

First-Aid Supplies for the Home

Adhesive tape ½ to 1 inch wide
Ace bandage
Antidiarrhea agent* (Kaopectate)
Antiseptic cleanser (hydrogen peroxide or Betadine solutions)
Antiseptic cream to apply to minor cuts and burns
Band-Aids
Calamine lotion
Cotton balls
Ice pack
Ipecac syrup* (to induce vomiting)
Cough syrup*
Baby aspirin*
Infant or child liquid Tylenol*

Roll of gauze
Ointment for rash
Rubbing alcohol*
Thermometer for children (rectal)
Petroleum jelly
Scissors
Tweezers
Separately packed sterile gauze pads
Medicine measure cup: Great! Put the medicine in a small measured
    cup and the child drinks it. No more spills from child pushing a
    medicine-filled teaspoon.
Humidifier or vaporizer

*Check with your pediatrician before using.

Resource Books

- *First Aid for Kids* by Susan Ann Johnson (Quick Fox, 1981).
- *A Sigh of Relief: The Revised Edition of the First-Aid Handbook
  for Childhood Emergencies* by Martin Green (Bantam, 1984).

Safety Tip

- Always check with your pediatrician before giving your child
  any medication!!!

Personal Safety Training for Children

Certain values that we fostered in children when they are young might
be detrimental later if they were faced with an adult authority figure
who was to harm them. If simple ground rules are established from
the very beginning, though, children will learn to distinguish between
appropriate and inappropriate behavior from authority figures. The
following ground rules were developed by S.A.F.E., The Safety and
Fitness Exchange, a wonderful organization dedicated to teaching personal safety to children.

   Your child has the right to physical privacy. The child's body is
theirs. Respect your baby/child if he doesn't want to be kissed, hugged

or touched by family friends or relatives. I don't know how many times I would force my children to hug or kiss relatives that they didn't want to. It is important to foster the idea that the child is entitled to judge who he wants to have physical contact with.

Your child has the right to say NO to authority figures. They have the right to question an authority figure. What do you mean?.... How come?.... Help your child learn to reflect on what is being said. You will have many situations to develop this type of thinking. Many adults will say silly things to your children. I remember one baby-sitter telling Marc that if he didn't hold her hand when crossing the street, the hand would fall off. Or if you eat too much candy your teeth will fall out. Ask your child, "Does that sound right?" This begins the process of helping your child evaluate statements or commands from adult authority figures.

Always explain a babysitter's rules in front of the sitter and children. Never say, "Listen to the sitter or do what the sitter tells you to do," but rather, "I want you to follow my rules that we just talked about." Permit your child to use the phone to call you.

I am not implying that children should be disrespectful to adults, but it is important that we raise our children to feel that it is okay to assert themselves with adult authority figures when they are in a situation that doesn't feel good or doesn't make sense to them.

When your child gets older, parents and teachers can provide more direct information on personal safety training.

S.A.F.E. gives lectures and sets up programs on a nationwide basis for community groups. You can reach them at this address:

> S.A.F.E.
> 541 Avenue of the Americas
> New York, N.Y. 10011
>
> (212) 242-4874

The following book will also help you give on-going training in personal safety to your children.

> *Your Children Should Know*
> by Flora Colao & Tamar Hosansky
> Berkley Books

CHAPTER 7

Reliable In-Home Child Care

Locating a reliable baby-sitter or full-time child-care person is, despite rumors to the contrary, actually easier than finding a pot of gold. This chapter will tell you where to find, how to interview, hire and provide on-going supervision of in-home child-care personnel.

Baby-sitters

From time to time, a baby-sitter can provide parents and child with a welcome respite from daily routine, and also offer both a bit of independence. At first it may seem hard to find someone to trust with the children who up until now have been solely your responsibility, but eventually you'll be able to negotiate your way through the baby-sitting network and find sitters who are especially capable and trustworthy.

Baby-sitters are usually teenagers, students, or mature persons who play with children, supervise homework, pick up children from school, or bring them to appointments. Usually no housekeeping is involved, but some sitters are expected to clean up after the children or get a few items from the grocery store. Also, if the baby-sitter is watching your child at mealtimes, she or he is responsible for preparing the food, serving, and cleaning up. Most sitters work part-time and are paid by the hour.

It is ideal to develop a list of qualified sitters with different strengths for different sitting assignments. Putting children to sleep, for instance, requires different experiences and maturity from supervising an after-

noon in the playground, bathtime, dinner plus bedtime. My son's favorite sitter for the evenings was a high school junior who was on the wrestling team. My favorite baby-sitter for long afternoons or when one child was home sick, was Mrs. Freed, a warm, grandmotherly person.

Where to Look for Baby-sitters

- Local hospitals with nursing students. Ask for nurses' residences or the nursing administrative offices.
- Colleges or universities. Try dormitories or placement services.
- High school placement services.
- Local Y's. Some have parenting programs with baby-sitter files.

- Professional schools. Many aspiring artists, musicians, actors, and so on supplement their income with baby-sitting jobs.
- Employment agencies with child-care divisions.
- Check Yellow Pages under Nurses, Baby-sitting, Child Care, or Employment Agencies.
- Post notices in supermarkets, banks, nursery schools, senior citizen centers, a community bulletin board, churches, and synagogues.
- Ask other parents.
- Check neighbors with teenage children.

What to Look for in a Sitter

The ideal sitter is a warm, responsible individual who enjoys children and will play with them. He or she should also be able to implement your rules in a friendly, good-natured manner. Sometimes it is hard to find a 15- or 16-year-old available on a weekend evening. Younger teens with young brothers and sisters, however, are often capable and responsible as sitters for older children. If you have an infant, you may feel more secure hiring a sitter who has experience with babies.

What to Ask Before You Hire a Sitter

Ask potential sitters about their previous sitting experience, age, grade in school, interests, hourly rate, and means of transportation. It may be you! Also request two current baby-sitting references and check them out. Questions for the references:

- How long have you known _____? How many times has he or she sat for you?
- What are the ages of your children?
- Does he or she come on time?
- What does he or she do with the children? Do they play, read stories, help with homework, color, play with blocks, watch TV, and so on?
- How does he or she show good judgment?
- Does he or she follow your instructions?
- What were the sitter's responsibilities? Preparing meals, bathing, putting to bed, taking child to playground, picking up from school, and so on.
- What are his or her strong and weak points?

If you feel comfortable with the responses, invite the sitter to spend a couple of hours with you and the children. This kind of informal meeting will ease the first baby-sitting assignment for all of you. For more detailed information on hiring a care giver, see Chapter 7.

Preparing the Sitter

- Have a new sitter come at least 30 minutes early.
- Show him or her where things are in your home (first-aid supplies, the fuse box, child's pajamas, and extra set of keys in case they get locked out).
- Make your family's rules clear, such as what TV shows are allowed, what snacks are okay, what time the children will go to bed, whether he will have a bath, etc.
- Explain your routines (for example, you might say that your child gets a 5-minute warning before an activity ends, then brushes his teeth, goes to the bathroom, gets a story read to him in bed, has a glass of juice, and sleeps with the lights on).
- Give specific instructions on what to do if your children refuse to cooperate.
- Mention your child's behavior characteristics that bear watching ("John puts everything in his mouth...").
- Leave emergency numbers by the phone (nearest hospital, pediatrician, police and fire department, ambulance, taxi).
- Leave information about where you can be reached (place, address, phone).
- Give the sitter the name and phone number of a nearby friend or relative who will be home (call first to see if they are available).
- Instruct sitter that no one is to be allowed into your home under any circumstances without your permission.
- Let your sitter know how you feel about his or her having guests.

Baby-sitting Co-ops

For free baby-sitting, organize or join a co-op. Members baby-sit each other's children, and one person keeps a record of the time worked and used by each member. Parents can make the arrangements together or designate a "secretary" to work out a schedule. Those seeking baby-sitting services usually ask a member of the co-op who owes time.

Child Care

One of the hardest things that I have faced as a parent is making arrangements for child care. For as long as I could, I just relied on baby-sitters, even after I started working part time. When no sitters were available, I balanced school and after-school activities with my work schedule—or took a feverish son to an important meeting and left him with the receptionist, my heart and stomach turning cartwheels while the rest of me made a presentation.

Finally, I faced the fact that I had to negotiate my way through the maze of child-care options, arrangements, and backup arrangements. Eventually I did find a long-term solution to my child-care problems. I hope that some of the facts I learned in the process will help make *your* search for good child care easier and your choices more assured.

Starting to Think About Child Care

- *Do you want individual or group child care?* First, think about your child's personality. Does he or she need a one-to-one relationship, or will he continue to thrive in a group situation that offers peer interaction (children can be very loving and giving with each other), stimulating materials and activities, and interplay with the staff. Some school-age children love after-school activities, whereas others need to unwind or relax in their own home or in a low-keyed setting.
- *What is your budget for child care?* Don't forget to consider transportation expenses when comparing costs of different child-care arrangements. Child care outside the home is not as expensive as in-home child care, however, as a rule.
- *What are your other household responsibilities?* It might be cost-effective for you to hire someone who will also do housekeeping, food shopping, taking children to after-school activities and appointments, cooking, and so forth.
- *What is the availability and accessibility of child care in your neighborhood?* First you must determine what the child-care options are in your community. If you are driving, explore what the parking situation is. The closer your destination is to home or work, the more convenient. If your child is near your place

of employment, you may be able to see him or her at lunchtime, and participate more frequently in parent/child activities.

Using a Combination of Child-Care Arrangements

For example, one mother returned to work when her daughter was 3 years old and her son was 7. She arranged for the 3-year-old to be in nursery school from 8:30 A.M. until 12, and at the school's extended day program. She hired a baby-sitter to pick up the child at school at 2:30 P.M., they both went to pick up the 7-year-old from school, and all went home together.

The Backup Plan

You always need an alternative plan for child care. Be prepared to juggle arrangements when baby-sitters get sick, children get sick and can't go out, the program is closed for a holiday, and so forth. There is never a single perfect solution.

Child Care in Your Home: Advantages

- Your child has the benefit of a one-to-one relationship with the sitter.
- He or she will have the comfort and security of a familiar home.
- If the child is sick, you need not make alternate child-care arrangements.
- You may tailor the hours of your sitter to your needs.
- You won't have to transport your child to and from the day-care center or sitter's house.
- Your care-giver may also clean house, cook, shop, and such.

Disadvantages

- The great range in competency of care-givers.
- Other children may be inaccessible.
- If the sitter is sick, other arrangements must be made.
- Limited selection of educational materials and equipment.

- If the sitter quits, you'll have to begin the search all over again and your child will have to readjust to a new sitter.
- In-home child care is expensive.

In-Home Care-Givers

- Nannies or nursemaids devote the majority of their time toward caring for the child. They rarely have housekeeping duties, but they are usually responsible for cleaning the child's room, doing the child's laundry, and fixing his or her meals. This type of child care is usually the most expensive ($175 to $350 per week and up). Although nannies should have experience in caring for children, very few have received formal training at the Nanny School in England. Those that have charge $275 per week and up.
- The housekeeper has responsibilities that vary depending on the age and needs of your youngster. She usually handles child care, housekeeping, cooking, shopping, taking children to appointments, and other chores. Costs will vary, but usually range from $175 per week and up. Can live in or live out.
- Au pairs live in your home. They help care for your children and perform housekeeping chores in exchange for room and board. Often, a modest salary is included. The au pair is usually a student or young adult who wants the opportunity to live in America. Most of their visas are limited to one year. Expect to provide close supervision and to pay for their medical expenses and round-trip fare. You can ask various employment agencies if they arrange placement of au pairs. Another suggestion is to ask other mothers that have obtained au pairs how they made their arrangements.
- Mother's helpers are usually students or young adults between jobs. In large urban areas, many young people who are trying to establish themselves in a career seek mother's helper positions. They take care of housekeeping and baby-sitting chores in exchange for room and board and perhaps a modest salary. Close supervision may be necessary.
- Relatives may care for children, which can be a very rewarding experience for all concerned. It is important, however, that you have confidence in a relative's child-care methods, and feel comfortable about explaining the ways that you would like things done. If there are major differences that can't be worked out, it is better in the long run to select another child-care option.

Give yourself enough time to hire a qualified person, familiarize him or her with the job, and help your child adjust to the new situation. It is important not to feel pressured. Expect to spend three to four weeks exploring and hiring, and then allow for a one to two week "breaking-in" period for your baby-sitter and your child (children) before you return to work.

How to Go About Finding In-Home Child Care

- Talk to other parents who you feel have hired excellent baby-sitters. Find out how they went about obtaining their child care, and ask if they know of any (available) sitters.
- Ask other baby-sitters who you know and respect if they could recommend a sitter.
- Contact licensed employment agencies that specialize in child care. Find out how long they have been in business. Explore their screening process (do they check references by telephone or in writing?). How far back do they check the person's work background? Ask about their fees: Is there a commission, a percentage of salary, or any agency fee? You can find a listing of these agencies in your classified telephone directory under employment agencies, sitting services, baby-sitters, or nurses.
- Call religious organizations.
- Many Y's that have parenting programs or toddler classes might have a listing of baby-sitters.
- Put a classified advertisement in a newspaper. See the next page for suggestions on how to write an ad.
- Put up a notice at pediatricians' offices, nursery schools, community bulletin boards, supermarkets, and so forth. See page 116 for suggestions on how to write a notice.
- Call up local hospitals with nursing students and nurses aides. Ask for the nurse's residence or the nursing administrator. Inquire if they have a listing of people who are available to baby-sit on a part-time basis.
- Check placement offices at local colleges or universities. Put up notices in dormitories.
- Call women's residences (sectarian and nonsectarian). Ask for the administration office.
- Call local high schools (public, private, and sectarian). Ask for the guidance counselor or administration office.
- Call professional schools (art, music, dance, secretarial, drama, etc.). Ask for the administration office or the placement office.
- Check women's organizations.

- Team up with another mother and hire a full-time person. Together you provide a full-time work schedule, but divide the time.

Writing a Classified Ad for a Child-Care Worker

Be brief but to the point. Spell out the specifics of the job. Better to have fewer calls, but candidates who are interested in the job you are looking to fill. Much easier on you!

The classified ad should be three to four lines.

Adjectives to Describe the Sitter

warm	mature	eager-to-	friendly
young	experienced	learn	female
energetic	hard-	patient	male
honest	working	neat	
intelligent	professional	conscientious	

Type of Care-Giver

housekeeper	student
baby-sitter	child-care
nanny	person

Child (Children)

number	characteristics:
ages	active,
sex	quiet,
	shy,
	friendly,
	energetic

Description of the Position

hours	some	light house-	live out
full-time	weekends	keeping	plain cooking
part-time	mainly child	housekeeping	driver's license
some	care	live in	
evenings			

Example for Your Classified Ad

Housekeeper Wanted

Warm, intelligent housekeeper to care for 2 active boys
ages 4 and 8. Friendly, harmless garter snake kept in locked
tank. Mainly child care with light housekeeping.
Some evening hours. A driver's license a must.
References required. (212) 874-2231 (day); 595-6632 (evenings).

Don't specify salary, leave it open for discussion during interview.
Place your classified in a newspaper with the kind of neighborhood,
ethnic, religious, metropolitan readership you want to reach—for example, an art or theatrical paper for more calls from the creative type.

A Bulletin-Board Notice for Child-Care Help

Use the same ad. Just repeat the phone number on strips of paper
that can be torn off.

Deciding What You Want In an In-Home Care-Giver

When you are hiring a full-time sitter, you have to decide what
type of person you feel comfortable with in sharing the raising of your
children. When you live in the city and frequent the playgrounds (as
I have done for the past eight years), you observe many child-care
people interacting with their charges. Looking around, you might say
to yourself, "I hope I can find someone like that when I go back to
work." Conversely, you may think, "Someone should tell that child's
parents what a terrible sitter they hired."

Two key factors to consider as you search for full-time child care
are: the age of your child, and the length of time you hope the person
will remain in your employment. When my children were younger, I
wanted someone who had a lot of energy and patience, and enjoyed
being with and playing with children.

At this point, I would be looking for a good listener who is warm,
willing to take the kids to after-school activities and ready to set limits
on homework, junk food, and television. The following guide will help
you determine what qualities to look for.

CARE-GIVERS FOR CHILDREN

Age of Child	General Traits of Child	Qualities of Care-Giver
Newborn to 6 months	Can sleep a lot. Can be quite fussy. Explores the world through seeing, hearing, and touching experiences.	Patience. Knowledge of and experience with young babies. Flexible. Does not have set ideas regarding handling of newborns. Holds, cuddles, kisses, and hugs the baby, and provides a variety of experiences such as singing, playing, and walking and sitting in playgrounds or parks. Most young babies love to hear and see other children.
6 months to 1 year	Baby begins to sit up, crawl, climb, and put everything in mouth. A real explorer. Baby is also beginning to show an interest in feeding himself.	Is loving, energetic, and understands the need for children to explore. Not overly concerned with cleanliness and order. Shows good judgment; knows to keep a constant eye on the exploring baby. Able to stimulate the baby and supportive in the baby's efforts to walk, talk, and play.

CARE-GIVERS FOR CHILDREN (*cont.*)

| 1 year to 3 years | On the go (walking, running, talking). Learning social skills; dealing with friends. Discovering how things work.

Struggling with dependence vs. independence conflicts. Wants to do things for self (like dressing and eating), yet wants to be taken care of.

Learning to use the toilet. | Intelligent, articulate, warm, and loving. Enjoys encouraging child's curiosity and answering the thousands of questions that spring from your little one.

Because your child is learning to talk and express himself, you need a sitter with a good command of the native language.

Because your child is learning through play, you want a playful, imaginative sitter who has patience to read stories, take walks, provide new experiences, and supervise outdoor activities.

Sitter must also be willing and able to take child to play dates or recreation programs, supervise play dates at the house, organize activities, and help children to negotiate when problems occur. If the sitter is friendly with other sitters in neighborhood, it will broaden your child's circle of friends. |

CARE-GIVERS FOR CHILDREN (*cont.*)

4 to 6 years	Busy making friends and learning about the world beyond their doorstep. Struggling between being a big (girl/boy) at school and desires for being a baby again. Testing limits.	Enjoys reading to child and playing games. Can supervise play dates, and can direct and balance other activities (outdoor, TV, indoor, friends). Helps child with the transition of coming home from school. Gives hugs or pats. Can provide comfort when nothing seems to be going right. (A friend won't share, or child wasn't picked to pass the juice in school, or a special TV program was missed, etc.)
7 years and up		Good listener. Gives space and respect for independence within realistic limits. Sets limits in a way that child will accept. Is able to implement rules for homework, TV, play, snacks, etc. Plays games. Supervises dates.

Important qualities of a care-giver when you have more than one child are:

- Should be energetic and able to divide time between both children.
- Organizes activities that encourage children to play together.

- Can coordinate disparate schedules and appointments for each child.
- Should be a good, imaginative negotiator who can deal effectively with children's continuous arguments.
- Attempts to be fair to each child.

Before the Interview

Once you have made contact with potential care-givers, you will need to interview them and check references, even if the names came from trusted friends or respected employment agencies. I used to be calm about interviewing prospective workers—until they walked in. So I decided that a little more preparation was in order.

Following are some ways to prepare yourself for the interview.

Step 1. Make a Task List

Make a list of tasks that need to be done on a weekly/monthly basis. Decide who will be responsible for what. Your list might look like this:

TASK LIST

Task	Mother	Care-Giver	Other
For the child			
Preparing breakfast			
Getting child washed and dressed in the morning			
Preparing lunch			
Thorough cleaning of child's room—making bed, changing sheets, organizing toys, dusting, vacuuming, laundry and ironing, organizing drawers and closets			
Bathing and preparing children for bedtime			

TASK LIST (*cont.*)

Task	Mother	Care-Giver	Other
Shopping for the child—clothing, birthday presents for friends, things for school, shoes, etc.			
Taking child to school			
Picking child up at school			
Transporting child to and from lessons, friends, parties, dentist, doctor, etc.			
Arranging play dates			
Taking child to park, playground, or for walks			
For the family			
Light housekeeping—washing breakfast dishes, making beds, straightening rooms, putting toys away, etc.			
Heavy housekeeping—bathrooms, kitchen, defrosting refrigerator, clean stove, vacuum, washing and waxing floors, etc.			
Limited grocery shopping			
Main food shopping			
Laundry and ironing for family			
Taking clothes to cleaner			
Preparing dinner for family			
Errands			

Remember! As children grow their needs change and therefore the sitter's assignments will shift to meet the changing needs. Example: While children are infants and toddlers the baby-sitter may not have much time for housework. When the child attends nursery school, however, the baby-sitter will have time for some household responsibilities.

Stress the need to be flexible.

Step 2. Make a List of Specific Questions

To assess the qualities and attitudes during the interview, always ask specific questions rather than general ones. For example, a general question would be,
"How do you feel about cleanliness?" A more specific question would be,
"What would you do if David, age 18 months, insisted on feeding himself and was getting most of the food on his clothes, the high chair, and the floor?"

The following examples might help you formulate your own questions for the interview.

What would you do if Karen threw a toy in anger and broke it?

Suppose Susan, age 2, cried every time she woke up from her nap? And what if she then became quiet, stubborn, and refused to come out of her room?

Jenny, age 2, is toilet trained, but usually wears a diaper when she takes a nap. How would you handle it if, one day, she refuses to allow you to diaper her?

Suppose Josh, age 18 months, runs all over the playground, attempting to experience all of the equipment?

How would you handle it if Karen, age 1, was putting everything she picked up in the house and in the backyard in her mouth?

Suppose Jane refused to eat her lunch?

What would you do if you asked Marc, age 4, to help pick up his toys and he refused?

Suppose you told Michael, age 4, that it was time to turn off the TV and take a bath, and he said, "I'm the boss of me, not you," and he turned the TV back on?

What would you do if you told Mary, age 5, that she couldn't have another cookie and she took one behind your back?

How would you handle Kara, age 3, if each time you picked her up from nursery school she cried that she hated you and wanted her mommy?

When you are preparing dinner, what will the children be doing?

What are your plans for the children when they come home from school?

How would you organize a game with 3-year-old Larry and 6-year-old David?

What would you do if Larry and David began to fight and David punched Larry?

What would you do if Larry and David wanted to watch different TV programs?

What would you do if Larry wanted to go to the playground but David wanted to stay home?

What would you do if Jenny, age 5, has a friend over after school and they got into an argument?

What ideas do you have for lunch and snacks?

What would you do if Matt, age 2, ran ahead and didn't stop at the corner?

What would you do if Susan had a friend over and refused to share her toys?

What would you do if Charlie wasn't using a ball that he brought to the playground and a friend of Charlie's asked you if he (the friend) could play with the ball?

Suppose Jimmy pushed a child and the child got hurt?

What would you do if Jon was being disrespectful to you and not listening?

Suppose you felt that Susan was not acting like herself for several days?

Step 3. Be Ready to Give a Realistic Description of Your Child's (Children's) Positive Points as Well as Negative Points and to Describe Your Methods of Dealing with Specific Behavior

Some areas that you might want to cover are:

- Child-rearing techniques (feeding, weaning from the bottle, toilet training).
- Manners.
- Discipline—your expectations for the sitter. Be specific.
- Responsibilities of the child (dressing, putting toys away, putting clothes in the hamper, etc.).
- Attitudes toward physical cleanliness and household order.
- Ways your child is permitted to express anger.
- Limits on your child's expressions of anger.
- Dealing with unacceptable behavior such as temper tantrums, physical aggressiveness, and lying.
- Punishment.
- Coping with fears and anxieties of children.
- In addition, explain the checks and balance systems between siblings. Discuss how you deal with things as:

Being fair	Privacy
Teasing	Friends over
Fighting	Sharing

It is impossible to find the "perfect" sitter. Some compromising is necessary. Realistically weigh what is negotiable and nonnegotiable. Do you want someone like you or someone who might complement your style, but not necessarily imitate it? You might consider hiring a person who possesses most of the attitudes and qualities you are looking for, but who has limited child-care experience. You also might be willing to overlook the fact that a candidate's child-rearing techniques are a little old fashioned.

Remember: Your style of child rearing can be learned. A person who is eager to learn and is open to suggestions can easily acquire excellent child-care skills. You just have to make a commitment to ongoing supervision.

Step 4. Know the Mechanics of the Job

When you hire a sitter, you become an employer who is responsible for social security payments and perhaps, workmen's compensation insurance (check the laws in your state).

Treat the sitter as you would like to be treated on a job situation: Clearly outline the sitter's wages, hours, and benefits (sick leave, holidays, vacations, etc.). These guidelines may be helpful to you:

Salary: Any sitter who works more than 20 hours a week should be paid at least the minimum wage. To find out what the going rate is, telephone your local State Employment Agency, or inquire at an agency that specializes in child care. Pay periods should be regular and means of payment should be agreed upon, in advance. Wages should be increased at least once a year.

Hours: Think realistically. If, for example, you expect to be gone from 8 A.M. to 4 P.M., make the sitter's hours 7:40 A.M. to 4:20 P.M. This will give you some time to meet with the sitter and exchange information and instructions. Also, explore the possibility of some evening hours. It is helpful if you can count on the same person who sits during the day to watch your children when you go out at night.

Overtime: Live-in workers should earn 1½ times their hourly rate for work done in excess of 40 hours a week; twice the rate after 48 hours.
Full-time, live-out workers should earn 1½ times the hourly rate after 48 hours.

Social Security: Employers must report earnings of employees. You must deduct their share of social security taxes from their wages and make equal payment for your share of their social security payments. Some employers pay both their share as well as the employee's as a benefit. The employer's share of social security cannot be deducted from employee's wages! (See Appendix.)

Tax Benefits: There is no distinction between child care inside or outside the home. Whether you use a sitter, day-care center, or nursery school, you can receive tax credits. Tax credits are also given for after-school and camp programs for children in grades 1 and up. For further information, write to the Internal Revenue Service (Request Booklet 153) or ask your accountant.

Insurance Coverage: Each state has its own regulations for insurance coverage for household workers. Many states hold the employer liable if:

- The sitter is injured on the job (whether or not neglect was involved).
- The sitter becomes disabled (ill or injured) on or off the job and can't work.
- To find what you are liable for as an employer of household

workers, ask your insurance broker or call the State Workmen's (Worker's) Compensation Board or a major insurance company in your community.

- Even if your state does not require you to purchase insurance, it is advisable to take out a homeowner's insurance policy to cover yourself if an accident occurs in your home. If you have no insurance, you might be personally liable for the full amount of an injured care-giver's medical and supportive expenses.

Benefits: Because your sitter is such an important resource to you and child, she or he deserves to be provided with realistic benefits. *Never skimp on your sitter.* The following are baseline benefits that most workers get automatically during the first year of their employment. These guidelines were developed by the National Committee on Household Employment: The National Urban League, Inc.

Vacation: Two weeks. The same for live-in or live-out help. For part-time baby-sitters, their vacation should equal at least two days a year for each day per week worked. Discuss with the sitter so you can determine a mutually convenient vacation time.

Holidays: Live-in sitter should have eight holidays; live-out sitter should have six holidays. Legal holidays are: Election Day, Thanksgiving, Christmas, New Year's Day, Memorial Day, Easter, Labor Day, Fourth of July. There are also religious holidays to consider. Before deciding which holidays to select for the sitter, check your work calendar and your children's school calendar to see that you are covered.

Sick Leave: Minimum of one day of paid sick leave a year per week-day worked. Example: Worked five days a week therefore entitled to five days a year. Develop a list of backup sitters of neighbors who may be available for days your sitter is absent.

Severance Pay: Depending upon the circumstances for termination of employment. Usually the employer pays two weeks.

Carfare: Decide if you will pay carfare to and from work.

Setting Up the Interview

When you get a call in response to your ad, always clarify the position on the telephone. If the applicant is still interested, arrange for an hour appointment. You might feel more comfortable to have another's opinion, so plan a time when both you and your spouse can be home, or ask a friend or neighbor to join you. You need not involve the child at this point.

It's also a good idea to inform the candidate on the phone to come for the interview prepared with specific information: employment history, names, addresses, and phone numbers of employers, dates of employment, plus names and phone numbers of references.

During the Interview

First, *have the applicant fill out the Child-Care Questionnaire.* The form might seem too formal, but it may help you obtain necessary information about the applicant without asking so many questions. It also shows the reading and writing proficiency of the prospective sitter.

CHILD-CARE QUESTIONNAIRE

Name_____

Address_____

Telephone_____

Children_____Ages_____Where are they_____

Educational Background

Last Grade Completed_____ Where_____

_____

Any Courses in Child Care_____

Explain Briefly_____

_____

Work Experience (Please account for past 5 years)

Employer_____

Address_____

Telephone Number_____

Dates Employed_____

Explain Briefly Job Responsibilities_____

_____

Reason for Leaving _____

_____

Employer _____

Address _____

Telephone Number _____

Dates Employed _____

Explain Briefly Job Responsibilities _____

_____

_____

Reason for Leaving _____

References(2) _____

_____

Name _____

Address _____

Telephone Number _____

Relationship _____

Name _____

Address _____

Telephone Number _____

Relationship _____

Notes _____

_____

_____

_____

_____

Getting the Answers from Former Employers

Past employers are often hesitant to answer questions frankly if they think they will hamper their former employees' chances of a job. Checking references involves careful and perceptive listening. Feel comfortable in persisting until you are sure that a reference has been honest and open with you. Always check at least two references. When asking questions about a sitter try to get an idea about the employer. Does this person share your ideas about child care? Your impression of a former employer will help you evaluate the applicant.

Questions to Ask Former Employers

- Review the factual information on the questionnaire to see if it is correct. Ask for dates of employment, child-care and household responsibilities, reason for leaving. Clarify any discrepancies.
- Ask how they found the sitter.
- Was she good in emergencies?
- How many days was she sick? Did she notify them when she couldn't come? Was she late, or usually on time?
- Was she honest?
- How did she handle her charges when they broke rules or didn't listen?
- Did she watch TV or use the phone a lot?
- What were her best points? What were her weak points?
- Would they hire her again?
- Did she have a lot of energy or did she tire easily?
- Child-care responsibilities (find out ages of children).
- How did the sitter handle problems involving the employer, the children, the schedule, and so forth?

Then follow through with Steps 1 to 3 on pages 120–24. You'll be well prepared to:

- Go over the tasks and responsibilities.
- Ask specific questions.
- Describe your child and the methods of child rearing you prefer and expect.

Finally,

- Ask if the candidate has any questions.
- Ask if she's interested in the position.

- If yes, discuss salary, benefits, and mechanics of the job (see Step 4 on pp. 124–26).
- Ask permission to contact references.
- Give a starting date and let the applicant know when you will make a decision.

At the end of the interview, you might want to reimburse the applicant for carfare.

Deciding Who to Hire

It may be impossible to find someone with all the traits you desire. Remember, though, that good child care can be taught, if the caregiver is open to your suggestions, and you must feel comfortable training her.

If you have mixed feelings or unanswered questions after the interview, invite the candidate back and introduce her to your children. How do they interact? If you still can't make up your mind, look around for another sitter. Never feel that you have no other options. You always do!

Familiarize Your New Sitter with the Job

Don't expect the sitter to know. Explain everything in detail: your child, the house, the neighborhood, and so forth. Discuss the child's likes and dislikes. I always told sitters that my youngest child liked his cheese put on his plate in a certain way, that he preferred softened ice cream, and he was used to being covered when he took his nap. Things like this are helpful in easing the sitter into her relationship with your child. Share anything you can think of. Give the sitter a tour of your home, pointing out how things work and don't work (washing machine, dryer, plumbing, fuse box, fire extinguisher, etc.) and where things are stored (clothing, cleaning supplies, first-aid supplies, toys, sporting equipment, bikes, etc.). Explain all house rules.

Show the sitter the local playground, museum, shopping, cleaners, and so forth. Arrange for a play date during this orientation period to familiarize the sitter with the routine. Go through the daily schedule as the sitter watches, then let her take over many of the chores.

The sitter should have on hand specific information, such as the address of the Y where the children go for after-school classes, the location of the school and the name of the teacher, and the address and phone number of the pharmacy. You might want to use the form, developed by Gloria Norris and Joann Miller, in *The Working Mother's*

Complete Handbook (Plume, 1984). Fill in the information and leave it in an accessible place. It will help your new sitter and ease your mind.

Emergency Situations

- Discuss who to call and what to do in dealing with an emergency. Always leave money in the house in case taxi fare or medicine is needed, or if emergency repairs must be made. Go over procedures for bleeding, choking, and poisoning. Emphasize safety rules that you want enforced. If you have a local Red Cross Chapter nearby, you might think of enrolling your sitter in a first-aid course during her working hours.

Touch Base Weekly

After you, the sitter, and your children have established a routine, you will still want to set aside time with her to discuss the events of the week, work out problems, and plan for the next week. Tell the sitter that you want a detailed rundown of what has happened. "Everything was fine" never tells the whole story. There are always ups and downs. If you know what's happening with your children, you can talk about their week with them, discover their new interests, and focus on problem areas.

Evaluating Your Sitter

For your own peace of mind, try to obtain reports on how the sitter is doing. Your child's teacher can tell you how your child reacts when he or she is dropped off or picked up by the sitter. Ask friends and neighbors their opinions of the sitter. You might also arrive home a bit earlier than planned once in a while, and make an unexpected visit to the local playground. This way you can get a firsthand idea about your sitter's involvement with your child.

Your Relationship with the Sitter

Children feel more secure when they are getting the same messages from the important adults in their lives. For effective communication between you and your sitter:

- Designate a place for notes, letters from school, information regarding after-school programs, notices, telephone messages, information about play dates, shopping lists, reminders, and so forth (use a bulletin board, file box, or front of refrigerator).
- Establish clear lines of authority and responsibility. Who has the authority when both sitter and parent are home? What decisions and authority does the sitter have when parent is not around?
- Set aside time to talk about what's happening: new developments, play dates, school, and so forth. It is important to share information as well as opinions, and for your child to see that you communicate.
- If there is a pressing problem that either of you wants to discuss, there should always be time available at the beginning or end of the day (this time should not be after the sitter's contracted time).
- Pay special attention to how the child separates from you and the sitter.
- The sitter must support your attitudes and objectives in child caring and rearing. Beware of the sitter who tells a child: "I don't like to do this, but your mother said..." Make it clear that any complaints should come directly to you and must never be discussed in front of the child. Keep in mind, however, that you must listen to and try to understand the sitter's point of view.
- Establish rules of conduct regarding use of telephone, watching TV, smoking, and so forth. When sitter lives in, come to an understanding regarding privacy, when and where she can entertain friends, and such.
- False expectations—many times we as parents want the sitter to love our child. This is unrealistic, although sometimes there is a special match between a child and a sitter that evolves into love. In most cases, however, the best that can be hoped for is an enduring warmth and friendship between the sitter, child, and parents.

CHAPTER 8

Child Care Outside Your Home

Licensed child care outside the home is usually group-oriented. You can choose between the larger, more structured programs such as group day care, after-school centers, and nursery schools with extended day programs, or the smaller, more intimate family day-care homes. Let's look at the options.

Group Day Care

All-day or half-day care for your children. Public day-care centers are operated on a nonprofit basis and parents pay on a sliding scale. Private programs may be either profit or nonprofit. Some private nonprofit centers also base their fees on a sliding scale, according to your income.

Day-care facilities operated for profit are often called "learning centers." They should be investigated carefully. A day-care center's first concern should be service, not profit.

Day-Care Center Advantages

- Offers a stable setting and predictable hours of operation. Many are opened on holidays and during the summer. Calendar is geared for the working parent. Hours are usually from 8 A.M. to 6 P.M.
- Provides a support system for working parents. Opportunity to meet other working parents who live in nearby communities.
- Offers a child the opportunity for peer contact.

133

- Generally more economical than at-home care.
- Child learns to deal with a variety of children and adults.
- Often offers a variety of learning, recreational, and social experiences.
- Usually staffed by professionals in Early Childhood Education.
- Licensed and inspected by the state to meet certain health and safety standards. Each state or city has its own regulations.
- Siblings can attend the same center, because it serves preschool to school-age children.

Day-Care Center Disadvantages

- Does not provide the homelike atmosphere some children need, and minimum opportunity for privacy or one-to-one relationship with adults.
- Doesn't leave much time for special play dates at friends' houses.
- Fixed schedule that children must follow.
- Different program schedules may result in many children coming and going during the day.
- Staff usually changes shift at least once during the day.
- Fixed hours of operation may not coincide with family's work schedule.
- If your baby is sick, you will have to make alternative child-care arrangements.
- The majority of day-care centers only take children who are toilet trained.

Qualities to Look For in a Good Group Day-Care Program

- Staff trained and certified to teach children.
- A well-equipped facility that provides:
- Clean and safe housing.
- Sufficient toilet and washing facilities.
- Good heating, lighting, and ventilation.
- Ample indoor and outdoor space for play and rest, and a wide variety of safe, stimulating play equipment and materials.
- Child-staff ratio:
  One to five for children 3 to 4 years old
  One to seven for children 4 to 6 years old
  One to seven for children older than 6 years
- Rich program content—daily routines should include indoor and

outdoor activities. Rest, nutritious meals, healthful and stimulating learning experiences under qualified supervision. The program should give each child an opportunity to build relationships with other children and adults, while it engages him or her in interesting and challenging activities.

- Parent participation—good day-care program involves parents at every level, including policy making.
- Nutritional plan—well-balanced meals should be served to children who spend the full day in a center. The daily food plan consists of mid-morning, and mid-afternoon snacks, and a hot meal—a lunch and sometimes breakfast and/or a late snack or supper.
- Health care—a good center requires medical supervision. Every child should be required to have immunizations and periodic medical and dental checkups. Many centers have a nurse on staff and a physician on call.
- Meets local licensing requirements—to ensure at least minimal standards, a center should be licensed by the appropriate governmental agency in the community. This might be the health department, board of education, or welfare department. Licensing helps protect the health and safety of young children.

Your Evaluation Visit to the Day-Care Center: Talking with the Director

Spend at least 30 minutes with the director, exploring the following topics:

- How long has the center been in operation?
- What is their primary source of funding? When there is a cut, how does it affect the program?
- Is the program licensed, and by which agencies?
- What is the staff-child ratio in the classroom?
- What is the schedule for staff shifts?
- What are the qualifications of the director and the teachers?
- What is the director's philosophy toward day care? What role does he or she think it plays in a child's life?
- How are costs and payments handled? Is there a sliding scale or scholarships available?
- What are the arrangements for sick children?
- How are individual versus group needs dealt with? Do children have some opportunity for one-to-one contact with an adult?
- Is there a quiet time or time for privacy?

- What is the daily schedule like? Is it balanced between active play and quiet time, free play and scheduled activities?
- Are there any specialty (music, art, dance) teachers?
- How do they handle a child who refuses to participate in the scheduled activity?
- If there is a religious affiliation, how is it integrated into the program?
- How do they help facilitate a child's adjustment to the center?
- How do they recommend you prepare your child for his or her day-care experience?
- Are the children on different schedules (full day, half day, three-quarter day, or after school)? How are arrivals and departures handled? How many children in your child's group are on the same schedule?
- What is the role of parents at the center? What are your responsibilities?
- Are there female and male role models at the center?

Evaluate by Observing

Observe the classroom for at least 1 hour. Try to begin your visit the first thing in the morning so you can see how the children and parents are greeted and how separation is handled. Things to look for:

- How does the staff relate to the children?
- Are they relaxed? Do they look directly at the child and listen to him or are they busy looking around the room?
- Do they treat boys and girls in nonsexist ways? Do they kneel on the child's level to play with or talk to the child?
- Are they accepting of behavior rather than judgmental when dealing with an argument or fight between two children? How do they handle discipline?
- How does the staff deal with: (1) sharing toys, (2) the withdrawn child, (3) the aggressive child, (4) the fearful child?
- Do you hear a lot of positive reinforcement ("that looks good" or "a good try")?
- Does the staff interact with the children, stimulating their curiosity, or does the staff play a basically supervisory role, setting up supplies, putting things away, and walking around the room monitoring activities?
- Does the staff help the children in their interaction with each other?

- Do you hear frequent words of encouragement from the teachers?
- How does the classroom staff work together? When one teacher is busy with a problem in the class, does the other keep an eye on the larger group?
- Do the children seem happy and relaxed? Are they actively engaged in playing?
- Does the room have play areas, such as:

   Block corner: Large selection of blocks and accessories: cars, trucks, traffic signs, people, animals, community workers. There should be enough space for the children to build creatively with the blocks.

   Arts and crafts: Diversity of supplies. Table space and easels. Are the children's paintings displayed on the walls?

   Housekeeping: Miniature stove, cabinets, table and chairs, crib, high chair, pots and pans, dishes, plastic fruits and vegetables, dress-up clothes, a telephone, and so on. Is imaginative play encouraged?

   Nature corner: Are there animals in the classroom?

   Quiet area: A loft of floor space with pillows and a rug.

   Books: There should be a good selection of picture books.

   Sand and water table

   Manipulative toys for eye-hand coordination: Pegs, small blocks, puzzles, nesting toys.
- Is the material in good condition: Are pieces missing from puzzles, books ripped, clay dry, paint dry, brushes not clean? Games with missing pieces?
- Is the room large enough for the number of children? Are there enough table and chairs, crayons, scissors, and other supplies?
- Is the school well maintained?
   Good lighting
   Ventilation
   Clean rooms
   Toys neatly put away when not in use
   Accident-proof rooms

Transition Times During the Day

How are key periods in a child's day handled?

- Separation: Arrival and dismissal. What happens with the tearful child? How do the staff and parents interact? Is there time for communication?

- Lunch and snacks: Do the children eat in small, informal groups? Do the teachers encourage social interaction?
- Transitions: Changing from one activity to another is a sensitive time in group situations. There should be time to finish an activity and prepare for the next. How is cleanup dealt with? Do children move from one activity to another smoothly?

Where is the bathroom? Can children go to the bathroom whenever they need to?

Family Day Care

Licensed day-care mothers, most of whom have had some training in taking care of young children, are authorized to care for up to six preschoolers under the supervision of social service agency. The licensing agent interviews the care-giver and examines her home to verify that both meet state requirements.

Advantages

- Homelike atmosphere, familylike group.
- Publicly funded (sliding fee scale).
- Siblings can be cared for in the same home.
- Day-care mother may be able to drive children to and from school, appointments.
- Social service agency provides support to the day-care home: educational supplies, nutritious meals and snacks.
- Children placed in alternate home if day-care mother is ill.
- Better ratio of adults to children than a day-care center.
- More likely to accept infants and toddlers not yet toilet trained.

Disadvantages

Family day-care homes vary markedly in quality. Some are excellently run, whereas others are lacking in facilities, experienced care-giver, and so on. A warm, loving home can provide excellent custodial care for children. Investigate carefully in order to find the best place for your child.

Evaluating Family Day Care

Look for the same qualities that you would look for in a baby-sitter (see pp. 116–20). In addition, you must evaluate other factors important in a day-care home.

- Is the care area safe, spacious, and clean? If it is a licensed family day-care home, the safety and health factors have been checked.
- The number and ages of children in the home (including day-care mother's children). Are there space, supplies, and equipment for all of the children?
- Is there a place for each child to put his or her belongings? Is there a table and chairs to fit the height of younger children? What are the napping facilities? Is there a place for outdoor play (nearby playground or a backyard)?
- Is there a variety of age-appropriate toys, books, and supplies for creative play?
- Does the sitter serve nutritious meals and snacks?
- Does she plan activities with the children, or do the children just seem to watch TV and hang out?
- Does the day-care mother seem energetic enough to handle a group of active children?

After-School or Extended-Day Programs

Many of the things you would look for in a full day-care program are desirable in an after-school program. Other important factors include:

- The transition from school to an after-school program is easier if your child knows other children who attend the program.
- Children have been following a structured routine all day in school. An after-school program should have a flexible, relaxing atmosphere, not an extension of the school day.
- Balance between free time and interesting activities.
- Take note of the age range of children assigned to a group.
- Are there appropriate supplies and equipment for your child's group?
- Qualifications of staff.
- Is there a pickup service from your child's school to the center?
- Is the center open during school vacations and holidays?
- Is a snack provided?

- Are the bathroom facilities adequate?
- Are special activities (sports, crafts, swimming) offered?
- Is there a quiet time to do homework? Is tutoring available?

Nursery School

In addition to the matters outlined in pages 191–95, consider the following when you evaluate a nursery school for day-care purposes:

- Is there a balance between working and nonworking parents? If the majority of the children are picked up by their parents and your child is picked up by a baby-sitter, it may be difficult for your child. Also, if the majority of parents are working, meetings and activities that include parents will be geared for the working parent.
- What are the school hours? When does the school close for holidays and vacations?
- What are the responsibilities of parents? Can you handle them with your work schedule? Are they flexible?
- Do they have a vacation program or summer day camp?
- Do they have an extended-day program? How many children from your child's class remain for the extended-day program? How many new children will be introduced in the extended-day program? Any staff from the nursery school involved in the extended day? Who are the other staff? Who is in charge of the extended-day program?
- Look into the types of programs that are offered in the vicinity of the nursery school. If the nursery school doesn't have an extended-day program, the school might be located near an after-school center that has pickup service.

A Comfortable Choice

Child-Care Options Near You

Give yourself enough time to research, select, and prepare your child. Finding a comfortable choice usually takes from 2 to 4 weeks.

- Locate the agency in your state that licenses child-care programs (i.e., the Board of Health, a Child Development agency, the Department of Social Services or the Bureau of Licensing). Write or call the agency for a listing of day-care, nursery schools, and after-school programs in your neighborhood and near where you work.

- Inquire at community centers, churches, or synagogues. Many religious organizations operate full-day, after-school, and nursery programs.
- Contact the Y's (YMCA and YM and YWHA)
- Ask friends, other working parents, elementary school principal (public or private).
- Ask your pediatrician.
- Telephone parents' associations, women's resource centers, or organizations such as NOW. They may have a list of day-care centers on file.
- Look in the yellow pages of your telephone directory under child care, schools, education, social service programs, or nursery schools. For after-school programs and lessons, look up under the specific activities (guitar lessons, ballet, gymnastics, piano lessons, etc.).

Deciding on the Right Program

No program will meet all your requirements. You will have to compromise, but compromise effectively by choosing the factors most important to you. Use the following list to pick out what is most essential for you.

- Majority of children stay for the full day
- Arrivals and departures of children on different sessions kept to a minimum
- Small program
- Large program
- New facility
- Well-established facility
- Clean and spacious
- Balance between male and female staff
- Good outdoor and indoor facilities for active play
- Specialty staff
- Teachers are warm, friendly, and supportive, involving themselves with each child's individual adjustment
- Staff/child ratio small
- Good stock of supplies and equipment
- Neighborhood program convenient to get to

- Balanced schedule
- Academic focus
- Arrangements for sick children
- Nutritious food
- Breakfast served
- Dinner served
- Great deal of parental involvement in policy making
- Interesting selection of after-school specialty classes
- Director seems professional and aware of all aspects of the program
- Program takes into consideration child's need for privacy and some one-to-one contact with adults
- Low-keyed program mixed with some interesting activities
- Child knows some children who attend program
- Sliding fee scale
- Scholarship program

The bottom line is do you like the program? Would you like your child to spend the day there? Trust your feelings!

Parent Orientation

Each center should have a parent orientation meeting so that parents can learn about the program, ask questions, and state their concerns. Find out what the philosophy of the center is and how they'll work to make your child comfortable.

Staying in Touch with the Day-Care Program

It is your responsibility to keep in touch with the staff about your child's adjustment to the program. Don't count on "they will contact me if there is a problem." It is important, especially with preschool children, to know the daily happenings in your child's life. When parents share information with the teacher in the morning (e.g., "Tommy didn't sleep well," "Tommy's cousin came over for dinner last night and he didn't get to sleep until late," or "It was Tommy's younger brother's birthday and Tommy feels left out"), or when the teacher tells you about a great building or drawing Tommy made, or how much fun Tommy had in the play, or how Tommy got into a lot of fights, the child gets (feels the) continuity in his or her life between day care and home. It is also important that the child see the staff and his parents in a partnership based on mutual respect.

CHAPTER 9

Favorite Toys, Arts and Crafts, and Pets

Children are mini-explorers. Some of my most cherished memories are of my children and their creative play. I can still picture them pushing a special toy, experimenting with paints, and having serious conversations with our varied family pets. This chapter will give you an overview on toys, arts and crafts, and pets for your child to enjoy right at home.

Toys

One day at the playground, my 4-year-old, Marc, ran over to me with a brightly colored rattle that he had taken away from a baby. He told me that he wanted it for his birthday (which was 10 months away). I told him I would put it on his birthday suggestion list. Together, Marc and I went to return the rattle to the baby. As I watched Marc and the baby play, I realized that the right toy can stimulate a young child to explore and learn. The greatest learning experiences for the very young child come through interaction, sometimes with people, sometimes with toys, and sometimes with the two together.

With an overwhelming number of new toys coming out each year for infants, toddlers, and preschoolers, parents' selection is frequently determined by the advertising media or the latest fad rather than the quality of the product. That doesn't have to be the case, though.

The following guidelines will help you choose quality toys.

144

How to Recognize a Good Toy

- Is it age appropriate? Nothing is more frustrating for a child than to have a toy, game, or piece of equipment that is too advanced for his age or stage of development.
- Can the toy be used in a variety of play situations? With blocks, doll playing, bathtub, outside, imaginative play?
- Is the price of the toy worth the length of time it will be used?
- Is it sturdy? If a part is lost, can the game still be used? Can you replace the part or repair the toy?
- If space is a consideration, do you have room for the toy?
- Is the toy washable?

Renewing and Enriching the Toy Supply

The floor might be covered with dozens of toys and your child will still say, "I have nothing to play with." I have two suggestions for reacquainting your children with their old toys:

- Take half of the toys and put them away for a couple of weeks. It is amazing how receptive your child will be when they are taken out of the closet again. The toy supply can be continuously recycled this way.
- Occasionally I buy inexpensive toys to add a little spice to imaginative play: a set of miniature dinosaurs, an accessory for the dollhouse, a matchbox car for the toy garage, small traffic signs for the blocks, little action figures, or just a couple of empty cardboard boxes from the supermarket.

Quality Toys Versus Toys Children Request

I might not like the junky toy my child saw advertised on TV and wants for his birthday, but on birthdays and holidays I usually honor his request, if it is within the limits of safety and budget. At other times I restock the toy chest with basic educational toys and equipment that will stimulate play and new exploring. You won't see these toys advertised on TV, but you will find them in stores or mail-order catalogs that sell primarily to schools. Many of these stores will also sell to individual customers. Ask the local nursery schools where they purchase supplies and equipment or look in the Mail Order section of the Appendix for educational toys, equipment, and supplies.

Special Toys for Special Ages

Newborn to 3 Months

For the first three months your baby will be interested in seeing, hearing, and touching. He can't coordinate arm and leg movements with what he is seeing; he won't quite know how to reach out for specific objects. During this time, a toy must be in a baby's visual field to get his attention. It should awaken and sharpen his sense of sight and sound. Toys that stimulate at this age:

- Musical mobiles that hang over the crib or dressing table. They should be colorful, move, and play music when wound up. Some play music for 10 minutes.
- Cradle gym or hanging beads for the crib or carriage. The best are colorful, make sounds, and have movable parts. See if play gym or hanging beads are long enough to use later in the play-pen. Some gyms have large wooden beads that 2- or 3-year-olds can string or build with. There are also crib and playpen rods with various accessories that are developmentally sequenced.
- Soft, stuffed animals or dolls, small enough for your baby to hold comfortably when he is able to grasp objects (large stuffed animals or dolls can be overwhelming at this age). Look for toys that are easy to hold; move or make sounds; are colorful and soft; are machine washable and dryable; and are made of a variety of fabrics to provide different sensory experiences.
- At this stage, your baby won't be able to hold a rattle himself, but you can entertain him by shaking the rattle for him. Look for a colorful rattle with sound and some kind of movement. Prepare for the time when your baby *will* be able to hold it, and make sure it is easy to grasp and safe to chew on.
- Teething toys for chewing and sucking. Choose ones that can be easily cleaned.

3 to 7 Months

At this age, children begin to coordinate their eye-hand movements, and become aware of cause and effect: "If I touch that button it will make a sound." They observe what happens if you push, pull, chew, and so on. Toys of this period should do a variety of things. Some should be small enough to hold in baby's hand, doubling up as a teething toy. Larger toys can be hung from the crib or playpen. These toys will be used more when the baby is sitting up by himself. Some toys should be soft, others hard.

- Rattles
- Balls
- Mirrors
- Stuffed animals that move
- Push and pull toys

7 to 12 Months

Now your explorer is sitting up and beginning to move around. Your child likes to undo and do; take apart; open and shut.

- Milk carrier
- Soft material blocks
- Stacking toys
- Snap-Lock beads
- Nesting drums
- Plastic jar to empty and fill with toys
- Cuddly dolls or stuffed animals
- Wooden puzzles with sturdy hardwood knobs attached to each large piece
- Children will love many of your kitchen supplies, especially pots and pans with covers, empty coffee pots (make a great puzzle to take apart), assorted plastic mixing bowls.

12 to 24 Months

At this age, children like toys that move and can be moved. Here's a list of motion toys for your child:

- If your child is walking: push and pull toys (should be sturdy, brightly colored, and make sounds)
- Banging and hammering toys
- Climbing toys to increase physical motor development of experienced walkers and climbers
- Puzzles with four to five pieces
- Dolls

24 to 36 Months

Children want to know how everything in their immediate world works. Lots of imaginative play at this age.

- Realistic representations of actual objects: Kitchen ware (sink, cabinet, stove); pots and pans, dishes; tea sets
- Blocks for beginners: Wooden (small and large), cardboard blocks, bristle blocks
- Wheel toys (riding toys)
- Rocking horse
- Push and pull toys (realistic representations of actual objects: shopping cart, baby buggy, doll stroller, ice-cream truck, trucks, fire engine, tractors)
- Sturdy large plastic vehicles: trucks, fire engine, tractors
- Play sets: play family house, circus train, mini bus, nursery school, cash register, farm
- Sand toys: pail and scoop, sand wheel, sifter, molds
- Music makers: marching drum, toy piano
- Puzzles with five to seven pieces

- Manipulative toys: large Lego blocks, sorting boxes
- Turn toys: music boxes, clock radio, carousel, Jack-in-the-box, talking toys

3- to 5-Year-Olds

At this age, children love to dress up or build with blocks, creating their own stage with toys as their props and acquiring valuable knowledge through their play. They begin to understand similarities, differences, classifications, and whole/part relationships as concepts. This group likes quiet as well as noisy times and begins to show a preference for specific activities. Friends, nursery school, and advertisements can greatly influence them. They become great collectors of cars, Star Wars toys, Strawberry Shortcake Dolls, Cabbage Patch Dolls, and the latest fads.

- Vehicles: small metal cars, trucks, buses, small wooden trains with tracks and accessories
- Wooden blocks
- Accessories for blocks: traffic signs, people, vehicles, animals, dinosaurs
- Lincoln Logs
- Geometric blocks
- Plastic building blocks (small and large)
- Play sets: medical set, play desk, hospital, firemen, knights, Indian and cowboys
- Props for imaginative play: jewelry, pocketbooks, masks and makeup (4 years and up), supermarket (shopping cart, cash register, play groceries), disguise kit, set of hats, luncheon or tea set, pots and pans, housecleaning set, puppets
- Dollhouse: furniture and accessories (alternatives to dollhouse is a big barn, store, or a modular community)
- Fad toys and accessories: Strawberry Shortcake, Star Wars, Cabbage Patch Kids
- Manipulative toys: threading and lacing (beads, buttons, lacing boards), Tinkertoys, pegs and pegboards, geometric boards, workbench
- Puzzles with 8 to 15 pieces
- Musical toys: marching band instruments, tape recorder, record player and records
- Science toys: magnet, little greenhouse, magnifying glass, butterfly net
- Board games

Board Games

There are several factors to consider before you introduce board games to your children. Do they understand the rules and concepts of the game? Are they emotionally prepared to deal with winning or losing? Can they manipulate the pieces? Can they concentrate for the length of time it takes to play? Can they wait their turn? Are they familiar with such concepts are left, right, forward, backward, up, down, and diagonal?

Board Games Recommended for Four- and Five-Year-Olds

Candy Land by Milton Bradley Co.
Candy Land Bingo by Milton Bradley Co.
Chutes & Ladders by Milton Bradley Co.
Cootie by Coleco Ind. Inc.
Mr. Mouth by Gabrielle Toys
Card games
   Lotto—simple classifications sorting skills (animals,
      fruits and vegetables, community workers, etc.)
   Memory by Milton Bradley Co.
   Card Matching
   Pick-up Sticks
   Old Maid
   Go Fish

Tips for Storing Board Games

The game boxes always fall apart, resulting in missing pieces and stained, torn boards. Organize your own storage system for board games. Buy plastic containers to store the game or put the parts in small plastic bags. Cover the board with a coat of shellac or plastic varnish before using. The boards will last longer and you can clean them with a damp cloth.

Sports Equipment

Always follow the manufacturer's recommended age for use and directions.

- Tricycle for 3-year-old, or a two-wheel bike with training wheels for a 4-year-old.
- Large soft rubber ball

- Ice skates
- Roller skates
- Floor punching bag
- Indoor gym
- Tumbling mat

Riding Toys for Toddlers (14 months–3 years)

There are two types of riding toy made for toddlers. The first kind is the type that the child pushes his feet against the ground to move. The second is the kind that moves by the child pedaling the riding toy. You should only buy the riding toy that your child pushes his feet against the ground to move rather then the one that has pedals because children do not start to pedal with ease until they are between the second and third year.

Tips on Buying Riding Toys for Toddlers

- Once your baby is secure in walking independently, you can begin to think about buying a riding toy that will provide lots of fun and exercise.
- Always take your child with you to try out the riding toy. Look for the following qualities:
  Well-balanced
  Sturdy
  Easy for your child to get on and off
  Easy for your child to control speed
  Easy to maneuver; does not turn over easily

Tricycles and Bicycles with Training Wheels (2½ years and up)

Between 2 and 3 years, your child will learn how to pedal and might want to try a tricycle or a two-wheeler with training wheels. Many parents are not buying tricycles but instead they purchase the smaller 10- or 12-inch two-wheeler bicycle with training wheels. This bicycle can be used until your child is 7 years old, but then will need a larger bicycle.

Regardless if you decide on a tricycle or a two-wheeler with training wheels, you should remember the following tips when selecting a bike or tricycle.

Tips on Buying Tricycles or Bicycles

- Ball-bearing parts instead of nylon; it makes the wheels move freely.
- Always buy a bicycle with your child so you can fit the child to the bike. The bike *must* fit the child. Never buy with the idea that your child will grow into the bike.
- See that the seat is wide enough and comfortable.
- Handlebars should be wide so that your child doesn't have to lean over to use.
- The bike should be easy to use. Give the bike a push to see that it rolls freely.
- The bike should be assembled only by professionals who know about bikes.
- Buy bikes from merchants who know about bikes—either from a toy store that has a large selection of bikes or from the bike store. They should have a repair shop so the bike can be adjusted to fit the unique needs of your child.

Removing the Training Wheels

At about 6 years, you can begin to remove the training wheels. Buy a box of Band-Aids and a dark pair of sunglasses for yourself so your child can't see the fear in your eyes while he is learning to practice without his training wheels.

Arts and Crafts

Arts and crafts have always been a favorite activity of my children, and I have enjoyed encouraging their creative endeavors. The key to success with arts and crafts is to maximize the enjoyment and minimize the creative mess. Both require patience and practice. I know that's true, because I learned the hard way.

Four years ago, it was my turn to host our 2-year-old's play group. Erik wanted to have play dough for his friends. I had the flour, salt, food coloring, water, rolling pins, and cookie cutters all ready when the four other 2-year-olds arrived. We started from scratch, dutifully measuring, mixing, kneading, and shaping. After 1 hour, the children were a mess, the house was a disaster, and I was a wreck!

However, when my second son, Marc, wanted play dough for his group, I was ready. This time, I put a plastic drop cloth under the table and covered the table with newspaper. As each child arrived, I gave them a cookie cutter and a ball of the blue play dough I had prepared the night before. Hassle was kept to a minimum and Marc's little friends went home happily with baked play dough designs.

There are numerous outlets for your child's creativity outside the home. In many communities, you can find delightful craft classes for toddlers and after-school workshops for older children. Visits to museums offer another opportunity to share a creative experience with your child. Despite your reminders not to touch, climb, or run, your children will probably marvel at the wonders in local galleries. But there's no substitute for the fun a child can have at home with paints, crayons, and clay!

Less-mess Home Craft Hints

- Always check to be sure the items you have chosen are nontoxic and recommended for the age of your child.
- Keep clean! You can buy your child a smock or make your own from one of your old shirts.
- Keep a stack of old newspapers to cover the floor and table.
- For a particularly messy project, cover floor and/or table with a clear piece of vinyl.
- A plastic tray like the ones used in cafeterias is a great idea for limiting your kids' work space when they're using crayons, Magic Markers, or finger paints. Stray marks and mess stay on the tray, off the floor and table.
- Use a wooden drying rack for hanging wet paintings, collages, and such.
- When water-based Magic Markers dry out because the tops were left off, soak them for 10 minutes in a cup of warm water.
- Find a separate place to store arts and crafts supplies. Keep scissors, paste, paint, out of the reach of young children.

The Basics—Supplies to Buy and Try

Scissors

- Buy a sturdy, easily maneuvered pair. The plastic ones, or ones that are difficult to open and shut, will only frustrate your child. Special scissors are available for left-handed children.

Paint

- Use only tempera paint. It's nontoxic and washable.
- Red, blue, and yellow can be mixed to create other colors. Use black and white to lighten and darken.
- Save money by buying large quantities of paint in liquid or powdered form from an art-supply store. The small commercial paint sets have only enough paint for one or two uses.
- Prevent undue mess by transferring paint onto small plastic palette or to empty juice cans. Another idea: spillproof containers with holes in the top for paintbrush dipping. Available in art-supply stores.
- Use only one color at a time for 1½- to 2-year-olds; 2½- to 3½-year-olds can handle two. At about 4 years old, children can begin to mix colors.

Paper

- As an economy measure, buy paper in bulk; 9 × 12 is good for coloring or drawing, 18 × 24 for painting. High-quality stuff is not a necessity. Children can go through a great deal of paper so it is a good idea to have a large supply on hand. For painting try newsprint, and for coloring and drawing try manila.

Brushes

- Buy long, fat, pointed camel-hair brushes, one for each basic color. Keep brushes point-side-up when drying.

Special Supplies for Different Ages

As children's fine-motor coordination improves, they can handle increasingly sophisticated implements. The following supplies are recommended for specific age groups. You'll accumulate quite a selection as your child grows older.

1½ to 3 Years

- Crayons—the jumbo size
- Finger paint and special finger paint paper, freezer wrap, or the shiny side of wax paper
- Chalk and blackboard. Children love making things appear and disappear

- Play-Doh or Plasticine (a type of soft clay that does not dry out)
- Thin white glue and brush for pasting
- Stamp and pad for printing

3 to 5 Years

- Black paper and white chalk
- Sewing materials like cardboard, a thick needle, and yarn (4 and up)
- Regular-size crayons
- Coloring books for developing hand-eye coordination
- A sturdy, double-sided easel
- Watercolor paint sets (4 and up)
- Construction paper
- Pipe cleaners
- Masking and Scotch tape in table dispensers
- Ice-cream sticks
- Real woodworking tools (5 years and up).
- Small looms for weaving potholders, etc. (5 and up)

Mail-Order Supplies

Buy good-quality supplies. If you have a hard time finding them in your community, ask a local nursery school where they purchase their materials. Contact the following companies for catalogs:

F.A.O. Schwarz
745 Fifth Avenue
New York, NY 10151
(212) 644-9400
Catalog is free.

Pearl Paint Co. Inc.
308 Canal Street
New York, NY 10013
(212) 431-7932
Catalog is $1.00.

Carol School Supplies, Inc.
185-04 Union Turnpike
Flushing, NY 11366
(212) 454-0050
Catalog is free

Childcraft
Catalog Department
20 Kilmer Road
Edison, NJ 08818
(800) 631-5652
Catalog is free. Ask for
"Toys that Teach" catalog.

Polk's Model Craft Hobbies, Inc.
Mail Order Department
314 Fifth Avenue
New York, NY 10001
(212) 279-9034
Catalog is $2.00 plus postage.

Simple Do-At-Home Projects

Brighten up a rainy day or cheer a sick child with these simple craft projects (or try them just for fun!).

- Paint pasta and paste it onto cardboard or string it together to make a necklace.
- Paper plate masks. Use crayons or magic markers to draw the face. Tie a string through a hole on each side of the plate and, *voilà*, you have a mask.
- Cut out pictures from magazines or old greeting cards and make a collage.
- Trace your child's hands and feet. Color and cut out. If you have a large enough piece of paper, try tracing your child's outline and help color or paint.

More Ambitious At-Home Crafts

When you and your child are looking for a truly challenging endeavor, try one of these more difficult projects: with patience, the results will be satisfying.

PLAY DOUGH

You'll need:

2 cups flour
1 cup salt
1/3 cup oil

3/4 cup warm water (for colored play dough add 1/4 cup tempera paint to water or food coloring)

1. Mix first 3 ingredients. Knead mixture until it is the consistency of cookie dough.
2. Refrigerate until chilled.
3. Dust work surface with flour.
4. You're ready to play! Roll, cut out designs with cookie cutters, or just model the dough into different shapes and objects. Play dough will last for approximately 5 days if kept in a closed container or plastic bag in the refrigerator.

DOUGH ORNAMENTS

You'll need:

4 cups flour   *1½ cups cold water*
1 cup salt

1. Mix all ingredients and chill.
2. Dust work surface and roll dough to about ¼ inch thick.
3. Use cookie cutters to make shapes or cut out letters to spell your
   child's name. Decorate (by embossing designs, etc.) before baking.
   If you want to hang the ornaments, remember to make a hole in
   the dough shape before baking.
4. Bake at 350° for 15 minutes or until edges turn light brown. After
   cooling, paint or shellac to preserve.

PAPIER-MÂCHÉ

Good for children 6 years and up.
You will need:

Newspaper   *Aluminum foil*
Paste (see following recipe)   *Drying rack*
Empty cans, cardboard tubes,   *Tempera paint*
* boxes to use as forms*   *Shellac*

1. Tear newspaper into strips and soak in thin paste until it is soft and
   pliable. Then apply in crisscross layers to can or other form.
2. An alternate method: Make a papier-mâché pulp by tearing newspaper into small pieces and soaking overnight in water. The next
   day, drain off the water and mix paper with paste until firm enough
   to model. Use pulp like clay, shaping without an underlying form,
   or apply by the handful to a selected shape.
3. Make animals, cars, or whatever your child's imagination and dex-
   terity dictate. To create detail, mold foil into desired shapes and
   attach to form before applying three layers of papier-mâché.
4. Let dry for a day, then paint with tempera paint, and shellac.

Paste

You will need: *1 cup flour*   Add water slowly until
               1 teaspoon salt   the mixture is gooey
               about ½ cup water but smooth.

Pets

My children have always loved animals and we have had a wide variety of household pets: a dog, fish, birds, lizards, a snake, gerbils, a tortoise, and a rabbit. The major responsibility for caring for young children's pets falls on the parents. Unless you have lots of time and love for animals yourself, buy a pet that requires little care until your child is old enough (about 9 years) to assume an active role in sharing the job.

Even pets that require a minimum amount of attention need on-going maintenance. Arrangements must be made for your pets when you go on vacation. If you have a dog, you might have to return home earlier than planned to walk him; or, you might have to shorten that long weekend because the rabbit needs to be fed.

Another fact that you and your children will face is the short life span of many animals. Our beloved Irish Setter, Autumn, died when Erik was 5 years old. He loved and missed her, especially at night when she had slept at the foot off his bed, warding off monsters and demons. However, the memory of his relationship with Autumn helped carry him through his mourning. When 2-year-old Erik's goldfish died prematurely after he took the fish out of the bowl to breathe, Erik was very upset and wanted to know what we were going to do with Goldie. I had been planning to flush the fish down the toilet, but decided against it when I recalled my own childhood feelings upon seeing my own little fish disappearing into the toilet bowl. Thank goodness Erik came up with a good solution: He got a box, filled it with sand, and laid Goldie in the box. He covered the box and gave it to our doorman to send to the Museum of Natural History!

We have had both "holding" pets and "watching" pets. Both provided enjoyable experiences. We would watch our goldfish endlessly as they traveled through the tank, and tried to engage them in a staring contest when they came close to the glass. But the holding pets, of course, can be cuddled. Even a very small pet can be taken from its cage and petted. Be prepared if your small caged animals escape from your grasp. We have spent hours searching for runaway gerbils.

To make a wise pet selection, know the facts about eating and breeding habits, life span, compatibility with existing household pets such as dogs or cats, number of times per week tank or cage must be cleaned, and other special characteristics. Remember, if you buy a bird, dog, or cat for your 5-year-old, you might still have the pet when your child is a teenager or away at school. If you have time and interest, pets are a wonderful addition to any family.

Here is a list of specific information on different pets for children:

Ant Farm

- Life span: 2 to 3 weeks.
- Equipment: Farm comes complete with food and order form for ants. Should be unbreakable and escape-proof.
- Feeding: Grass seeds or cornflakes once a week.
- Activities: Observe how ants dig tunnels and build bridges.
- Maintenance: Minimum amount of care. Can be left alone for one week. Order new ants or find your own.

Birds (Canaries and Parakeets)

- Life span: 7 to 12 years.
- Equipment: Cage, paper for the floor, feeder, water dish, beak conditioner, toys, gravel.
- Feeding: Prepared birdseed every day.
- Activities and tips: Watch birds play with their toys. Not easy to tame. Train them one at a time.
- Maintenance: Floor must be cleaned and water changed every day. Can be left overnight.

Fish in a Bowl

- Life span: Goldfish live up to 5 years; Siamese fighting fish, two years.
- Equipment: Wide-mouth bowl, gravel, plants, net for removing fish while cleaning bowl.
- Feeding: Fish food every other day or twice weekly.
- Activities and tips: It's more personal for the child to have fish in bowl rather than tank.
- Maintenance: Clean bowl once a week for fighting fish; goldfish, every 2 to 3 days.

Fish in Fishtank

- Life span: Depends on selection of fish.

- Equipment: Tank, pump, filter, heater, thermometer, light, gravel, plants, net.
- Feeding: Fish food every other day or twice a week.
- Activities: Observing school of fish; breeding fish.
- Maintenance: Clean tank once a year. Clean the filter when dirty, according to manufacturer's instructions.

Anole Lizards

- Life span: 2 to 3 years.
- Equipment: Glass aquarium with fitted, ventilated lid; floor covering of rocks, bark, small logs; warm light source (Vita-Lite), spray bottle.
- Feeding: Live food (crickets, worms, and mealworms).
- Activities: Watch lizards change colors.
- Maintenance: Live food obtainable at pet stores; must be purchased on a weekly basis. Clean tank once a month or when there is an odor.

Cats

- Life span: 15 years.
- Equipment: Litter box, litter, food and water bowls, toys.
- Feeding: Cat food and water once a day.
- Characteristics: Friendly, playful; can be petted and cuddled.
- Maintenance: Litter box must be cleaned every third day and stools removed from box daily. Veterinarian checkups once a year. Can be left overnight.

Dogs

- Life span: 15 years.
- Equipment: Leash, water and food bowls, hairbrush.
- Feeding: Once or twice a day. Water must be available at all times. Vitamins.
- Characteristics: Great companions for children.
- Maintenance: Must be walked at least three times a day. Need daily exercise, including a good run. Checkup at the veterinarian once a year. Can't be left alone overnight.

Gerbils

- Life span: 3 years.
- Equipment: Cage or tank with ventilated lid. Newspaper, sawdust, or sand to cover floor. Food bowl, water bottle attached to side of cage.
- Optional: An exercise wheel, long sticks, rocks.
- Feeding: Every other day prepared mix from pet store.
- Characteristics: Hardy and friendly; curious and playful. Odorless! Happy in pairs. Members of the opposite sex or sisters can be kept together. Males tend to fight. Many like to sleep during the day and play at night (remember this if your child is a light sleeper).
- Maintenance: Cage must be cleaned every 2 to 3 weeks. Water must be readily available in bottle. Keep gerbils away from drafts, dampness, excessive heat, and windows. Can be left alone for weekend.

Guinea Pigs

- Life span: 3 to 5 years.
- Equipment: Cage or tank with ventilated lid. Water bottle attached to side of cage, hay or sawdust to cover floor, food bowl that will not tip over. Branch to keep teeth trim.
- Feeding: Twice a day prepared mix from pet store plus green leafy vegetables.
- Characteristics: Chunky animals with friendly but somewhat timid disposition. Easy to handle. Females can be put together but not males.
- Maintenance: Floor must be cleaned daily to prevent odor. Can be left for only one night. Must be kept away from drafts.

Hamsters

- Life span: 2 to 3 years.
- Equipment: Cage or tank with ventilated lid. Water bottle attached to side of cage, sturdy food bowl, exercise wheel, ramps, ladders, and logs. Sawdust for the floor. Alternately: the Habitrail, a basic starter unit consisting of a living compartment and a loft

connected by a tube. Add to the basics and build a complete network of housing (like a burrow system) made of transparent tubes through which you can see your pet in action.

- Feeding: Prepared mix from pet store plus fresh green and root vegetables. Feed once a day.
- Characteristics: Timid, solitary animals that should live alone except when they are breeding. Active at night. Enjoy playing and exploring.
- Maintenance: Clean cage or tank at least once a week. Can leave overnight.

Mice

- Life span: 18 months to 2 years.
- Equipment: Cage or tank with ventilated lid, water bottle attached to side of cage, sturdy food bowl, sawdust for floor.
- Feeding: Prepared food mix from the pet store, nuts, and greenery. Feed once a day.
- Characteristics: Cheerful, need limited room, easy to tame, sleep during the day, active at night. The female can produce 4 to 18 babies in a litter. Female comes into season every 4 or 5 days.
- Maintenance: Clean bottom of cage at least twice a week; scrub whole cage thoroughly once a month. Can be left over weekend.

Rabbits

- Life span: 5 years.
- Equipment: Cage or hutch, sturdy food bowl, sawdust for floor, water bottle attached to side of cage.
- Feeding: Prepared rabbit pellets or mix, plus green leafy vegetables (not lettuce). Feed twice a day.
- Characteristics: Can live indoors or outdoors. Sociable and cuddly.
- Maintenance: Bottom of cage must be cleaned daily, thoroughly washed every month. Can be left overnight.

Tortoise

- Life span: 50 to 80 years.
- Equipment: Tank with newspaper or wood chips to cover the floor, food and water bowls, plus a rock or stick.

- Feeding: Once a day, a mixture of fruits or vegetables. Water available at all times.
- Characteristics: Solitary animals that can form relationships. If you let them out of the tank, it is interesting to watch them explore.
- Maintenance: Change newspaper on bottom of tank twice a week; scrub tank thoroughly once a month. Can be left over weekend.

Deciding on a Pet

- Go to a pet store. Find out the cost of the basic equipment for the cage or tank and add the weekly expense for food and supplies.
- If the pet is the kind you can hold, ask the salesperson if you and your child can handle it. Ask the salesperson to teach you how to pick up and hold the animal. Make sure you're comfortable with an animal before you buy it.
- Never buy the pet the first time you go to the pet store. Give yourself time to think it through. Don't give in to the first little furry creature you see.
- Before buying a pet, help your children plan who will be responsible for what. Even a young child can be assigned a little responsibility for caring for the pet.
- If possible, consult with another parent who has lived with the same type of pet.
- After you have made your selection, read about the type of pet you have chosen.

Good luck!

CHAPTER 10

Books, Magazines, and Music for Children

Erik always loved our special storytime together. Marc was thrilled by music. Our favorite trip was to the local library's children's room. Erik would settle down with a selection of books and magazines, while Marc put on the headphones and listened to a stack of records. Today, there is an extensive selection of books, records, tapes, and magazines available for children. The following recommendations should be helpful to you in introducing the world of books, magazines, and music to your child.

Books

Introduce your child to books at an early age. Even the very youngest ones can appreciate a picture book or a story read aloud. Unpressured reading for pleasure can open up new, exciting worlds for your youngster and foster a lifelong love of books.

Relaxed Reading Experiences to Enjoy with Your Child

- Make reading aloud something to look forward to. Don't let story time become a routine chore. On hectic days, forgo the story if you are too tired.

- Listen to a record or story cassette tape with your child. Available at most libraries, some have companion books so your child can "read" along with the spoken words.
- Limit your reading to one book or one chapter a night.
- Schedule regular visits to the library and take your child to story hours.
- Work together with your child on an activity book.
- Plan an early evening "quiet time" for the whole family. Write, read newspapers, magazines, books, mail, while your preschoolers look at picture books alone or with you. Try it, if only for 5 minutes.
- Ask your youngster to tell his or her own version of a picture story.
- Just pointing out and naming objects in a picture book is fun for little children.

- Don't stop reading to children after they learn to read. What you choose to read aloud may be intellectually stimulating, even though the reading level is beyond a child's reading skills.
- Join a children's book club to insure a continual source of reading material at a reasonable price. For a listing of book clubs, see the Mail Order section in the Appendix.
- Make note of your child's favorite books and search out others by the same authors.

Books for 6- to 12-Month-Olds

- Board Books. Books made of strong cardboard with a sturdy binding and rounded corners. Some board books can be cleaned with a damp cloth.
- Spiral bound books. Make sure that the plastic or metal spiral doesn't have an exposed sharp point and won't break off.
- Each page should contain a simple, realistic picture of familiar objects. Distorted images can be confusing.

Some Favorite Titles

- *Baby's First Book* by Margaret Borrett (Putnam, 1978).
- *The Apple* by Dick Bruna (Price Stern, 1984).
- *I Am a Mouse* by Geoffery Bull (Chr. Lit., 1975).
- *Wild Animals* by Tony Chen (Random House, 1981).
- *Baby's Lap Book* by Kay Chorao (Dutton, 1977).
- *My First Book of Things* illustrated by John E. Johnson (Random House, 1979).
- *Baby Animals* by Harry McNaught (Random House, 1976).
- *Farmer John's Animals* by J. P. Miller (Random House, 1979).
- *Friends; Family; Playing; Working; Dressing* by Helen Oxenbury (Simon & Schuster, 1981).
- *Puppies* by Jan Pfloog (Random House, 1979).
- *Baby Farm Animals* by Barbara Pichett (Western Publishing, 1983).
- *Looking at Animals; Going for a Ride; in the House; at the Table* (Price/Stern, 1980).
- *I am a Puppy, I am a Kitten* by Ole Risom (Golden Books, 1970).
- *Max's New Suit; Max's Ride; Max's Toys* by Rosemary Wells (Dial Books, 1979).
- *Nursery Rhymes* by Eloise Wilkin (Random House, 1979).

Books for 12- to 18-Month-Olds

- Children this age still enjoy board books.
- Books that depict children's activities.
- Touch-and-feel books or fold-and-unfold books or stretch-books. Curious youngsters like to find hidden things in a story.

Some Favorite Titles

- *Farm Animals* illustrated by Lisa Benforte (Random House, 1981).
- *Here's Spot* (1984), *Spot's First Walk* (1981), *Spot's Birthday Party* (1982), *Spot's First Christmas* (1983) by Eric Hill (Putnam).
- *Sleepytime Book* by Margaret Hillert (Golden Books, 1975).
- *Pat the Bunny* (1942), *The Telephone Book* (1975) by Dorothy Kunhardt (Golden Books).
- *Big & Little* by J. P. Miller (Random House, 1975).
- *One Nose, Ten Toes, If I Met a Dinosaur, If I Had a Parade* (Putnam, 1981).
- *Feed the Animals* (1944), *See the Circus* (1956), *Anybody at Home?* (1942), *Where's my Baby?* (1943) by H. A. Rey (Houghton Mifflin).
- *Touch Me Book* by Eve Witte and Pat Witte (Golden Books, 1961).
- *Animal ABC* illustrated by Patricia Wynne (Random House, 1977).

Books for Your 1½- to 2-Year-Old

- Illustrations should still be simple and realistic, with each page depicting only one simple concept.
- Begin to introduce paper books in addition to board books.
- Animals and children are favorite subjects.

Some Favorite Titles

- *A Child's Book of Animals* by Robert Allen (Putnam, 1981).
- *The Blanket* (1976), *The Cupboard* (1976), *The Dog* (1976), *The Friend* (1976), *The Rabbit* (1975), *The School* (1975), *The Snow* (1975) by John Burningham (Harper & Row).
- *Freight Train* (1978), *Harbor* (1982), *Carousel* (1982), *Truck* (1980), *Parade* (1983) by Donald Crews (Greenwillow)

- *Play with Me, Just Me* by Marie H. Ets, (Penguin, 1976).
- *Mother Goose, Come Out and Play, Make-Believe, My Animal Friend, 1,2,3, A Counting Book, Fairyland, Faraway Friends Year In, Year Out, Dreamland, Here I am, Good Morning, Puppies Pussycats and Other Friends* by Gyo Fujikawa (Putnam 1981).
- *Big Bird's Farm* (1981), *Grover's New Kitchen* (1981), *Grover's Monster Album* (1980), *Muppets in My Neighborhood* (1977) (The Sesame Street Series, Random House).
- *Animals in the Woods* by Michele C. Roosevelt (Random House 1981).
- *The Fire House* (1981), *The Food Market* (1981), *My School* (1981), *People* (1980), *The Pet Store* (1981), *The Toy Store* (1981) by Peter Spier (Doubleday).

Choosing Books for Your 2- to 5-Year-Old

- 2- to 3-year-olds enjoy simple stories or poetry. At this age your child will begin to appreciate finer details and enjoy illustrations with a lot of activity.
- Children can handle paper books easily now.
- Select books based on your child's rapidly budding personal interests.
- 3- to 4-year olds like books about the real world, featuring people at work and performing day-to-day activities.
- 4- to 5-year-olds enjoy humorous, scary, and reassuring books.
- 5- to 6-year-olds like books that play with words; try rhyming texts, riddle books, and poetry. They also delight in stories with strong plots, fantasy, well-developed characters, and detailed illustrations.
- Try fairy tales with your 5- to 6-year-old. By this age, children begin to distinguish between fantasy and reality. They love to hear about witches, giants, sorcerers, and magic. Always read the story beforehand to make sure that it won't frighten your child.

Some Favorite Preschool Titles

The following list of wonderful picture books for children was compiled with the help of school librarians, parents and children, and personnel from Eeyore's Books for Children in New York City (see Mail Order section in the Appendix). Ask your librarian about new and special interest books that your child might like.

• *Each Peach Pear Plum* by Janet and Allen Ahlberg. In this "I Spy" book, the child is asked to find a "hidden character" in each picture. The simple rhyming text and colorful illustrations are cheery. (ages 2–6) (Viking, 1979)

• *At Mary Bloom's* by Aliki. A story with a humorous twist about what happens when the girl next door tells Mary Bloom about her mouse's new babies. (ages 2½-6) (Penguin, 1978)

• *The Stupids Step Out* by Harry Allard and James Marshall. The Stupids are a family who don't seem to be able to get anything quite right. The children try to slide up the banister; Mr. Stupid wears his socks on his ears; they love mashed potato sundaes. Children revel in their own superiority to these slapstick clowns. (ages 4–8) (Houghton Mifflin, 1974)

• *Madeline; Madeline's Rescue; Madeline and the Bad Hat; Madeline and the Gypsies; Madeline in London* by Ludwig Bemmelmans. The adventures of Madeline, the smallest student in a boarding school for girls in Paris. (ages 4–8) (Penguin 1977)

• *Bear Scouts; Berenstain Bear Almanac; Bears' Christmas; Bears in the Night; Bears on Wheels; Bears' Picnic; Bears' Vacation; The Berenstain Bears and the Missing Dinosaur Bone; Big Honey Hunt; Bike Lesson; C is for Clown; He Bear, She Bear; The New Baby; The Berenstain Bears Go to the Doctor; The Berenstain Bears Visit the Dentist; The Berenstain Bears' Moving Day; The Berenstain Bears and the Sitter* by Stanley and Janice Berenstain. These funny, rhyming books deal with the various adventures of this charming bear family. (ages 3–6) (Random House)

• *Goodnight Moon* by Margaret Wise Brown. A little bunny says goodnight to each thing it can see from its bed. A soothing story about going to sleep. (ages 2–6) (Harper & Row, 1972)

• *The Runaway Bunny* by Margaret Wise Brown. A reassuring story about a little bunny's plans to run away and its mother's love and understanding. (ages 3–6) (Harper & Row, 1972)

• *The Country Noisy Book* (1976); *The Noisy Book* (1939); *The Quiet Noisy Book* (1950); *The Summer Noisy Book; The Winter Noisy Book* (1976) by Margaret Wise Brown. These books encourage your child to assist Muffin the dog in identifying various sounds. (ages 2–6) (Harper & Row)

• *The Very Hungry Caterpillar* by Eric Carle. The baby caterpillar eats through anything he sees. Along the way, the readers learn the days of the week, numbers 1 to 5, the dangers of overeating, and the process of insect metamorphosis. (ages 2½–5) (Putnam, 1969)

• *The Babar Series* by Jean DeBrunhoff and Laurent DeBrunhoff. Babar the orphan elephant is cared for by the Old Lady and finally becomes king of the elephants. These elegant books are filled with the adventures of this delightful French elephant and his family. (ages 4–8) (Random House)

• *The Popcorn Book* by Tomie De Paola. Enjoyable story of two brothers' adventures popping popcorn one evening. Not only does the book explain how to pop popcorn, but it gives a charming factual account of the history of the snack. (ages 4–8) (Scholastic, 1979)

• *Michael Bird-Boy* by Tomie De Paola. A young, nature-loving boy is determined to find out the source of the black cloud that hovers above the countryside. (ages 4–8) (Prentice-Hall, 1975)

• *Are You My Mother?* by P. D. Eastman. While mother bird is out looking for food, baby bird hatches. Confused, he searches for his missing mother and finally finds her. (ages 4–8) (Random House, 1967)

• *The Story About Ping* by Marjorie Flack. A little lost duck spends a night alone on the Yangtze River. (ages 4–8) (Viking, 1977)

• *Corduroy* by Don Freeman. A very special department store bear finds the home he has always wanted with a little black girl named Lisa (ages 3–5) (Viking, 1968)

• *Pocket for Corduroy* by Don Freeman. The continuing adventures of Lisa and her teddy-bear friend, Corduroy. (ages 3–5) (Viking, 1980)

• *Millions of Cats* by Wanda Gag. An old man and woman decide that they want a cat. Unable to choose just one, the old man brings them all home. (ages 3–6) (Putnam)

• *The Funny Thing* by Wanda Gag. A man changes a dragon's diet from children's dolls to more nutritious things. (ages 4–8) (Putnam, 1952)

• *Mr. Books Series* by Roger Hargreaves. Mr. Bounce; Mr. Bump; Mr. Busy; Mr. Chatterbox; Mr. Clumsy; Mr. Forgetful; Mr. Fussy; Mr. Greedy; Mr. Grumpy; Mr. Happy; Mr. Impossible; Mr. Lazy; Mr. Messy; Mr. Mischief; Mr. Muddle; Mr. Noisy; Mr. Nonsense; Mr. Nosey; Mr. Quiet; Mr. Skinny; Mr. Silly; Mr. Small; Mr. Tickle; Mr. Worry. Each book personifies a different quality. (ages 4–9) (Price Stern, 1980)

• *Bear By Himself* by Geoffrey Hayes. A bear explores the pleasures of solitude. (ages 3–6) (Harper & Row, 1982)

• *Bedtime for Frances* (1976); *Baby Sister for Frances* (1964); *Birthday for Frances* (1976); *Best Friends for Frances* (1969); *Bread and Jam for Frances* (1964) by Russell Hoban. Frances, a young badger, goes through all the trials of growing up. (ages 4—8) (Harper & Row)

• *Rosie's Walk* by Pat Hutchins. Out for a walk, Rosie the hen doesn't realize that the fox is following her. She unwittingly leads the sly villain into one predicament after another. A humorous book for the very young. (ages 2—6) (Macmillan, 1968)

• *Changes, Changes* by Pat Hutchins. A little wooden couple rearranges a set of blocks into whatever the situation demands. No words to this story. (ages 2—6) (Macmillan 1973)

• *Don't Forget the Bacon* by Pat Hutchins. Distractions on the way to the store make it awfully hard to keep the grocery list straight. As new items are added, the shopping expedition becomes increasingly funny. (ages 3—6) (Penguin 1978)

• *Harold's Circus* (1981); *Harold's ABC* (1981); *Harold's Trip to the Sky* (1981); *Harold and the Purple Crayon* (1958) by Crockett Johnson. Harold is a boy with a remarkable crayon. Whatever he draws becomes real. Sometimes, if he isn't careful, he draws himself into trouble and has to do some quick thinking to draw himself out of it. (ages 4—8) (Harper & Row)

• *The Snowy Day* (Viking, 1962); *Whistle for Willie* (Penguin, 1977); *Goggles* (Macmillan, 1971); *Pet Show* (Macmillan, 1974); *Hi, Cat!* (Macmillan, 1971); *The Trip* (Scholastic, 1979); *Regards to the Man in the Moon* (Scholastic, 1981) by Ezra J. Keats. Simple stories with colorful and expressive illustrations. (ages 4—7)

• *There's No Such Thing as a Dragon* by Jack Kent. A boy finds a dragon in his house and no one believes him. The more his parents disbelieve, the larger the dragon becomes. (ages 4—7) (Golden Books, 1975)

• *Leo the Late Bloomer* by Robert Kraus. A little tiger blooms in his own good time. (ages 4—7) (Harper & Row, 1971)

• *The Carrot Seed* by Ruth Kraus. A little boy who believes, when everyone else doubts, that the seed he planted will grow. (ages 3—6) (Harper & Row, 1945)

• *The Red Balloon* by Albert Lamorisse. A photostory about the little French boy, Pascal, and his faithful red balloon. Based on the movie of the same name. (ages 4—8) (Doubleday, 1978)

• *The Story of Ferdinand* by Munro Leaf. Ferdinand is a Spanish bull who likes to sit and smell the flowers. Complications arise when he is selected for the bullfights in Madrid. (ages 4–8) (Penguin, 1977)

• *Alexander and the Wind-up Mouse* by Leo Lionni. The friendship of two mice—one real, the other a wind-up toy. (ages 4–7) (Pantheon, 1969)

• *Frederick* by Leo Lionni. Frederick the field mouse contributes his share to the winter stockpile in the form of poetry, food for the soul. (ages 4–8) (Pantheon, 1966)

• *Swimmy* by Leo Lionni. A clever little fish outsmarts the big fish and protects his school by organizing his friends into the form of a giant fish. (ages 4–7) (Pantheon, 1963)

• *George and Martha* (1972); *George and Martha Encore* (1973); *George and Martha Rise and Shine* (1979); *George and Martha One Fine Day* (1978) by James Marshall. George and Martha are hippos with buck teeth and a great friendship. (ages 3–7) (Houghton Mifflin)

• *Close Your Eyes* by Jean Marzollo. Story with lovely illustrations, about a father's efforts to lull his child to sleep (ages 2½–4) (Dial, 1981)

• *There's a Nightmare in My Closet* by Mercer Mayer. Would you climb into bed with your nightmare? The young hero of this book does just that when he finally decides to confront his fears. (ages 3–7) (Dial, 1968)

• *Blueberries for Sal* by Robert McCloskey. A mix-up occurs when Sal and her mother and Mother Bear and her cub both set out on a blueberry expedition on the same hillside. (ages 4–7) (Penguin, 1978)

• *Tikki Tikki Tembo* by Arlene Mosel. This book explains why the Chinese no longer give names to their children. With a rhyming text that kids love to chant. (ages 4–7) (Scholastic, 1984)

• *Rosie's Birthday Party* by Marietta D. Moskin. It's Mama's birthday, which leads Rosie to search for the best gift. One surprise follows another. (ages 4–7) (Atheneum, 1981)

• *The Little Engine that Could* by Watty Piper. The classic story of the train that must get over the mountain, and the little engine that saves the day. (ages 3–6) (Scholastic, 1979)

• *Peter Rabbit Books* (23 vols.) by Beatrix Potter. Miniature hardcover books reproduce her original illustrations. (ages 4−8) (Warner, 1981)

• *Curious George series* by H. A. Rey. The misadventures of an inquisitive monkey and his friend, the Man in the Yellow Hat. (ages 4−8) (Houghton Mifflin)

• *Sam Who Never Forgets* by Eve Rice. Sam the Zookeeper forgets to feed the elephants, and trouble ensues. (ages 3−6) (Penguin, 1980)

• *Goodnight, Goodnight* by Eve Rice. A bedtime book that's sure to give a young listener sweet dreams. (ages 3−5) (Penguin, 1983)

• *Where the Wild Things Are* by Maurice Sendak. When Max is sent to bed without his supper, he imagines sailing away to where the wild things are. Wilder than any of them, he quickly wins their respect and becomes king. But Max is lonely and wants to be where he is loved, not feared (ages 4−8) (Harper & Row, 1984)

• *In the Night Kitchen* by Maurice Sendak. A little boy visits the night kitchen where bread and cake for the morning are being made while the world sleeps. (ages 4−8) (Harper & Row, 1970)

• Dr. Seuss Books: *The Cat in the Hat; The Cat in the Hat Comes Back; Hop on Pop; Green Eggs and Ham; One Fish Two Fish Red Fish Blue Fish; The 500 Hats of Bartholomew Cubbins; And to Think That I Saw It on Mulberry Street; The Lorax; On Beyond Zebra!; My Book About Me; The King's Stilts; Yertle the Turtle; McElligot's Pool; Horton Hears a Who; Happy Birthday to You; Scrambled Eggs Super!; Dr. Seuss's Sleep Book; Horton Hatches the Egg; I Can Lick 30 Tigers Today! & Other Stories; The Sneetches & Other Stories; Thidwick: The Big-Hearted Moose; I Had Trouble Getting to Solla Sollew; Did I Ever Tell You How Lucky You Are?; How the Grinch Stole Christmas.* Books that play with rhyming words in an amusing way. (ages 4−9) (Random House)

• *Caps for Sale* by Esphyr Slobodkina. A tale of a peddler, monkeys, and monkey business. (ages 3−7) (Scholastic, 1976)

• *Sylvester and the Magic Pebble* by William Steig. Sylvester the donkey is accidentally turned into a rock, but the power of his parents' love transforms him into his old self again. (ages 4−7) (Windmill Books, 1969)

• *Amos and Boris* by William Steig. A little mouse is shipwrecked, but a giant whale saves him. Years later, the mouse returns the favor. (ages 4–7) (Penguin, 1977)

• *The Little Red Lighthouse and the Great Gray Bridge* by Hildegarde H. Swift and Lynd Ward. When a great bridge is built around the little lighthouse on the Hudson, the lighthouse suffers a loss of confidence. How it becomes useful again makes a lovely story. (ages 5–8) (Harcourt Brace Jovanovich, 1974)

• *Eloise* by Kay Thompson. Eloise is a little girl who lives at the Plaza Hotel in New York. She is not yet 7, but she is certainly a character. (ages 5–9) (Simon & Schuster, 1969)

• *My Mama Says There Aren't Any Zombies, Ghosts, Vampires, Creatures, Demons, Monsters, Fiends, Goblins, or Things* by Judith Viorst. Sometimes even mommies make mistakes. (ages 4–8) (Atheneum, 1973)

• *Alexander and the Terrible, Horrible, No Good, Very Bad Day* by Judith Viorst. As the title suggests, it's just not Alexander's day. (ages 4–8) (Atheneum, 1972)

• *Lovable Lyle* (1977); *Lyle, Lyle, Crocodile* (1973); *Lyle Finds His Mother* (1974); *House on East Eighty-Eighth Street* (1975); *Lyle and the Birthday Party* (1973) by Bernard Waber. Find out what happens when a crocodile moves in with a family living in a New York City brownstone. One adventure is more hilarious than the next. (ages 4–7) (Houghton Mifflin)

• *Ira Sleeps Over* by Bernard Waber. When Ira is invited to stay overnight at a friend's house for the very first time, he can't decide whether or not to take his beloved teddy bear. (ages 4–8) (Houghton Mifflin, 1975)

• *The Harry series* by Gene Zion. *Harry and the Lady Next Door* (1960); *Harry the Dirty Dog* (1976). The adventures of Harry, the lovable dog. (ages 4–7) (Harper & Row)

Fairy Tales

• *The Miller, The Boy and the Donkey* adapted by and illustrated by Brian Wildsmith (Oxford University Press, 1969)
• *Anansi the Spider: A Tale from the Ashanti* retold and illustrated by Gerald McDermott (Holt, Rinehart & Winston, 1972)

- *Arrow to the Sun: A Pueblo Indian Tale* by Gerald McDermott (Viking, 1974)
- *The Magic Tree: A Tale from the Congo* by Gerald McDermott (Penguin, 1977)
- *The Stonecutter: A Japanese Folk Tale* by Gerald McDermott (Viking, 1975)

The following fairy tales are available in many editions from various publishers:

- *Cinderella*
- *The Hare and the Tortoise*
- *Hansel and Gretel*
- *Jack and the Beanstalk*
- *Little Red Riding Hood*
- *The Monkey and the Crocodile*
- *Puss-in-Boots*
- *The Shoemaker and the Elves*
- *Snow White*
- *Sleeping Beauty*
- *Three Billy Goats Gruff*

Classics for Ages 5 and Up

Many children in this age group enjoy stories read aloud, even if there are no illustrations. I remember when my oldest son and I read Roald Dahl's *Charlie and the Chocolate Factory* (Bantam, 1979) together. We were so enthralled by the tale that we stayed up extra-late to finish the last chapter and find out who won the contest. After this experience, I began to look for other books to read aloud. Here is what I found:

- *Peter Pan* by James Barrie. The ever-popular story about Peter and Wendy and her brothers in Never-Never Land. (Avon 1982)
- *My Father's Dragon* (1980), *Elmer and the Dragon* (1980) by Ruth S. Gannett. About a brave boy and a young dragon is nonsense written so matter-of-factly as to be believable. (Dell)
- *Mrs. Piggle-Wiggle; Mrs. Piggle-Wiggle's Magic; Hello, Mrs. Piggle-Wiggle* by Betty MacDonald. What to do with a child who won't take a bath, eat, or go to bed. Distressed parents call upon Mrs. Piggle-Wiggle for her unconventional and imaginative answers. (Harper & Row, 1957)
- *Charlotte's Web* by E. B. White. A wonderful book about an intelligent and generous spider named Charlotte and her barnyard friends. (Harper & Row, 1952)

• *Stuart Little* by E. B. White. This adventurous and heroic little mouse searches for this lost friend Margalo, the beautiful bird. (Harper & Row, 1945)

• *The Trumpet of the Swan* by E. B. White. Louis is a swan who has no voice. To compensate for this handicap, he becomes a famous trumpet player. How he learns to do it and how he wins his love Serena make a heartwarming story. (Harper & Row, 1973)

The following classics are available in many editions from various publishers:

• *The Wind in the Willows* by Kenneth Grahame. The book that introduced Mole and Ratty and Mr. Toad to the world four generations ago continues to be popular with young readers. (ages 5 & up)

• *Winnie-the-Pooh* by A. A. Milne. These simple stories about Pooh the bear, Christopher Robin, Piglet, and their friends are timeless classics.

• *The House at Pooh Corner* by A. A. Milne. More adventures of Winnie-the-Pooh and his friends. Several of the stories feature the sometimes gloomy, but always lovable, Eeyore the donkey.

Science Favorites

• *Animals Do the Strangest Things, Reptiles Do the Strangest Things, Birds Do the Strangest Things, Fish Do the Strangest Things, and Insects Do the Strangest Things* by Leonora and Arthur Hornblow (Step-up Books by Random House).

There are other series of science and natural history published by Harper & Row ("Let's Read and Find Out" series), and Price/Stern/Sloan ("The How and Why Wonder Books"). Although these books are geared toward children who already read, they can also be enjoyed by younger ones, when a patient parent reads aloud.

Magazines

Kids love to receive their own mail—and what better way to guarantee a regular delivery than by subscribing to a magazine? They make great gifts.

Some are purely for fun, others sharpen reading readiness skills, and still others feature stories, puzzles, and suggestions for crafts, games, and projects.

Before selecting a magazine, review the children's periodicals at your local school or community library. A child who is already reading will probably enjoy selecting his or her own magazine. Here are some suggestions:

Chickadee

- Ages: Under 8 years
- Focus: Interests children in their environment and the world around them. Mix of stories and activities.
- Advertisements in magazine: no
- Address: *Chickadee*
  The Young Naturalist Foundation
  51 Front Street East
  Toronto, Ontario M 5 E 1B3

Highlights for Children

- Ages: 2 to 12 years
- Focus: Stories, projects, features, games, poetry, riddles, puzzles. Geared to a variety of age levels.
- Advertisements in magazine: no
- Address: *Highlights for Children*
  2300 W. 5th Avenue
  Columbus, OH 43216

Let's Find Out

- Ages: 4 to 7 years
- Focus: Stories and activities with built in early learning skills.
- Advertisements in magazine: no
- Address: *Let's Find Out*
  Scholastic, Inc.
  P.O. Box 644
  Lyndhurst, NJ 07071

Sesame Street Magazine

- Ages: 2 to 6 years
- Focus: Based on TV program. Stories, learning games, poems and craft projects.
- Advertisements in magazine: yes
- Address: *Sesame Street Magazine*
  P.O. Box 2895
  Boulder, CO 80321

WOW

- Ages: 4 to 9
- Focus: Stories, games, riddles, cut-outs, pop-ups, a surprise every time.
- Advertisements in magazine: no
- Address: *Wow*
          Scholastic Home Periodicals
          P.O. Box 1925
          Marion, OH 43302

Magazines as Read-Aloud Sources

There are publications—such as science or literature magazines—that have greater depth of subject information. These are excellent for introducing your child to intellectually stimulating materials by reading them aloud. As your child develops independent reading skills, these magazines are wonderful independent reading sources as well.

Cobblestone

- Ages: 8 to 13 years
- Focus: On American history for children, each issue focuses on a single theme (a person, place or event in American history) in order to thoroughly cover the subject.
- Advertisement in magazine: no
- Address: Cobblestone Publishing, Inc.
          P.O. Box 959
          Farmingdale, NY 11737

Cricket

- Ages: 6 to 12 years
- Focus: Wide variety of reading for every interest: folk tales, fantasy, tall tales, stories about real children and their adventures, science and nature, biographies of important people, serious poems, nonsense rhymes, riddles, puzzles, jokes and craft projects.
- Advertisement in magazine: no
- Address: *Cricket*, The Magazine for Children
          P.O. Box 2670
          Boulder, CO 80322

National Geographic World

- Ages: 8 to 13 years
- Focus: Factual stories about the real world, including natural history, science, child-oriented human interest stories, educational games, puzzles, and activities.
- Advertisement in magazine: no
- Address: *National Geographic World*
  National Geographic Society
  17 and M Street
  North West Washington, DC 20036

Odyssey Magazine

- Ages: 8 to 13 years
- Focus: Magazine of astronomy and outer space for children.
- Advertisement in magazine: no
- Address: *Odyssey Magazine*
  625 E. St. Paul Ave.
  P.O. Box 92788
  Milwaukee, WI 53202

Music

You don't have to be a family of opera stars to enjoy singing and rhymes. Even off-key singing or reciting a nursery rhyme while rocking my children helped quiet them at night. It also proved a useful tactic for keeping them still while changing or dressing them, and distracted them from their hunger while I prepared a bottle or food. Here are some old favorites to soothe your little ones:

Classic Lullabies and Rhymes

Hickory Dickory Dock

Hickory, dickory, dock;
The mouse ran up the clock;
The clock struck one,
The mouse ran down;
Hickory, dickory, dock.

Jack and Jill

Jack and Jill went up the hill
To fetch a pail of water;
Jack fell down
And broke his crown,
And Jill came tumbling after.

Old King Cole

Old King Cole
Was a merry old soul,
And a merry old soul was he.
He called for his pipe
And he called for his bowl
And he called for his fiddlers
   three.

Ring Around the Rosie

Ring around the rosie,
Pocket full of posies
Ashes, ashes
We all fall down.

Row, Row, Row Your Boat

Row, row, row your boat,
Gently down the stream
Merrily, merrily, merrily, merrily,
Life is but a dream.

Pop Goes the Weasel

All around the cobbler's bench
The monkey chased the weasel;
The monkey tho't t'was all in fun,
Pop! goes the weasel.

Rain, Rain Go Away

Rain, rain, go away.
Come again another day.
Little (name of child) wants to
   play.
Rain, rain, go away.

Rock-a-Bye Baby

Rock-a-bye, baby, in the tree top,
When the wind blows, the cradle
   will rock;
When the bough breaks, the cradle will fall,
And down will come baby, cradle and all.

Old MacDonald Had a Farm

Old MacDonald had a farm,
Ei-igh, ee-igh, oh.
And on that farm he had some
   (chicks).
Ei-igh, ee-igh, oh.

Chorus:
With a (chick, chick) here
And a (chick, chick) there.
Here a (chick).
There a (chick).
Everywhere a (chick, chick).

Repeat, using:
duck—quack
turkey—gobble
pig—oink
cow—moo
donkey—hee-haw

Pick a Bale of Cotton

You got to jump down, turn
   around
Pick a bale of cotton.
Jump down, turn around, Pick a
   bale a day.

Chorus:
Oh lawdy, pick a bale of cotton
Oh lawdy, pick a bale a day.

Teensy Weensy Spider

The teensy weensy spider
Crawled up the water spout
Down came the rain and washed
   the spider out
Out came the sun and dried up
   all the rain
So the teensy weensy spider
   climbed up the spout again.

I've Been Working on the Railroad

I've been working on the rail-
  road all the livelong day,
I've been working on the rail-
  road just to pass the time away.
Don't you hear the whistle blow-
  ing?
Rise up so early in the morn!
Don't you hear the captain
  shouting,
"Dinah blow your horn."
Dinah won't you blow? Dinah
  won't you blow?
Oh, Dinah won't you blow your
  horn, your horn.
Dinah won't you blow? Dinah
  won't you blow?
Oh, Dinah won't you blow your
  horn?

Humpty Dumpty

Humpty Dumpty sat on a wall,
Humpty Dumpty had a great fall.
All the king's horses
And all the king's men
Couldn't put Humpty together
  again.

Twinkle, Twinkle, Little Star

Twinkle, twinkle, little star
How I wonder what you are!
Up above the world so high,
Like a diamond in the sky.

See-Saw, Margery Daw

See-saw Margery Daw,
Jacky shall have a new master;
Jacky must have but a penny a
  day,
Because he can't work any faster.

Are You Sleeping? (Frère Jacques)

Are you sleeping, are you sleep-
  ing,
Brother John? Brother John?
Morning bells are ringing,
Morning bells are ringing
Ding, Ding, Dong,
Ding, Ding, Dong.

French version:
Frère Jacques, frère Jacques,
Dormez vous? Dormez vous?
Sonnez les matines,
Sonnez les matines,
Din, Din, Don,
Din, Din, Don.

Baa Baa Black Sheep

Baa, Baa, Black Sheep,
Have you any wool?
Yes sir, yes sir,
Three bags full;
One for my master,
One for my dame,
But none for the little boy
Who cries in the lane.

Farmer in the Dell

The farmer in the dell,
The farmer in the dell,
Heigh-o the derry-o,
The farmer in the dell.

Repeat, using:
The farmer takes a wife
The wife takes a child
The child takes a nurse
The nurse takes a dog
The dog takes a cat
The cat takes a rat
The rat takes the cheese
The cheese stands alone

Yankee Doodle

Yankee Doodle went to town
A-riding on a pony.
He stuck a feather in his hat
And called it macaroni.

Chorus:
Yankee Doodle, keep it up,
Yankee Doodle dandy,
Mind the music and the step,
And with the girls be handy.

Jingle Bells

Jingle Bells. Jingle Bells.
Jingle all the way!
Oh what fun it is to ride in a one-
    horse open sleigh—
Jingle Bells. Jingle Bells.
Jingle all the way!
Oh what fun it is to ride in a one-
    horse open sleigh!

Record Players and Tape Recorders

A child's record player is a good investment if your child enjoys listening to records. If budget is a consideration, however, think of the many uses of a tape-recorder. In addition to listening to prerecorded cassettes, the tape recorder can entertain your children when you are traveling in a car, train, or bus. Tapes can't get scratched. Children also love to hear themselves on homemade tapes. I would suggest that you buy a regular tape recorder, not one made especially for children. Buy a durable, easy-to-use model. Many libraries have an extensive selection of children's records and cassettes. A good resource is *Music for Ones and Twos* by Tom Glazer (Doubleday, 1983), a book of songs and games for the very young child.

Records and Cassettes

Children love listening to records and cassettes. A favorite story read aloud, or a sing-a-long can be an individual or family activity. A small selection of records and cassettes for children:

Pete Seeger

Abiyoyo and Other Story Songs
American Game and Activity Songs for Children
American Playparties
Birds, Beasts, Bugs and Little Fishes
More Birds, Beasts and Bigger Fishes
American Folk Songs for Children
Folk Songs for Young People
Golden Slumbers

Ella Jenkins

My Street Begins At My House
And One and Two
Early Childhood Songs
Little Johnny Brown
This Is Rhythm
Call-and-Response Rhythmic
Nursery Rhymes-Rhyming and Remembering
Jambo-and Other Call-and-Response Songs and Chants
You'll Sing a Song and I'll Sing a Song
Counting Games and Rhythms for the Little Ones
Adventures in Rhythm

Peter, Paul and Mary

Peter, Paul and Mommy

Raffi

Singable Songs for the Very Young
More Singable Songs
The Corner Grocery Store
The Cat Came Back
Baby Beluga

Woody Guthrie

Songs to Grow on for Mother and Child
Children's Songs, sung by Bob and Louise de Cormier

Tom Glazer

Music for 1's and 2's
Lets Sing Fingerplays
Happy Rhythms and Rhymes
Children's Greatest Hits, Vol. 1 and 2
Activity and Game Songs, Vol. 1, 2, and 3

Margaret Miller

Margaret Miller Sings Songs for the Early Years

Sharon, Lois and Bram

This group has records with children's songs from all over the world.

Hap Palmer

Series

Movies and Plays

Sound of Music
Mary Poppins
Annie
Finian's Rainbow
Star Wars
Chitty Chitty Bang Bang
Peter Pan
The Pirates of Penzance

Favorites

Really Rosie
Free to Be You and Me
Peter and The Wolf
Nutcracker Suite
Sorcerer's Apprentice

Favorite Series

Mr. Rogers
Sesame Street
Walt Disney
Danny Kaye Reads Hans Christian Andersen

Popular Stories Read Aloud on Records or Cassettes

A number of books listed in this chapter are also available in records and cassettes. Check at the library or your neighborhood toy or book store. Also check the mail order chapter for stores where you can order records and cassettes.

Read-a-Long Books on Records

Your beginning reader can follow along with the book as he listens to the record.

CHAPTER 11

Playing and Learning with Other Kids

Making friends and learning to work and play cooperatively in a group setting is an important aspect in your child's life. This chapter explores the full range of social experiences your child will encounter—from the neighborhood playground, to play dates, to nursery schools, to birthday parties, to day camps. The information in this section will help you plan, evaluate, and select appropriate social experiences for your growing child.

Activities for You and Your Baby

Over the past few years, many programs have been developed for babies and their parents. Activities such as exercise classes, swimming, gym, music, and support groups give you many chances to meet other parents with young children and help to lessen feelings of isolation, especially during the winter when cold weather limits outings.

A working mother or father whose schedule is somewhat flexible might be able to attend early morning, lunch hour, or weekend activities. Perhaps your housekeeper or baby-sitter would enjoy attending these activities with your child.

Locating Activities in Your Neighborhood

First, obtain names of programs by asking:

- Your pediatrician
- Other mothers of young children

- Local religious organizations
- Community centers
- Superintendent of Public Schools office
- Y (YMCA, YWCA, YMHA, YWHA)
- Lamaze chapter
  If you have difficulty locating local chapters, write or call their national offices to locate a chapter near you (see Appendix for addresses of the national organizations).
- Your representative to the state legislature. Call to find out what agency licenses infant, toddler, and early childhood activities in your city and state. Write to the agency and ask for a directory or list of licensed programs in your community.

Next, contact the programs and arrange to visit and speak with the person who will be teaching the class. If you like what you hear and see, find out their registration schedule and ask to be placed on their mailing list for other activities and programs for children.

Some activities are costly, whereas others are quite reasonable, so be sure to inquire about costs.

Activities for Your Toddler

Although 2- and 3-year-olds don't really play with each other in a give-and-take way, they seem to enjoy having other children nearby who are involved in similar play. Now and then, however, you will see children playing together for brief periods. The following situations allow children to engage in informal social contact with other children.

Playgrounds

In Manhattan, the neighborhood playground was my children's backyard. We would go on a regular basis and get to see the same children and parents. While watching and discussing whose toy belonged to whom, the parents had opportunities to laugh, to talk, and to share valuable hints and resources. Before long, play dates, picnics, and day outings were arranged, play groups developed, children signed up for the same swim and gym program, and valued information shared on baby-sitters, nursery schools, children's dentists, and so on.

My children and I made lasting friendships from our days at the playground. Many families still get together for picnics and Erik and

Marc have ongoing contact with many friends from their toddler days in the playground. Our playground experience provided us with a wonderful sense of community which we needed, living in a large city.

Playground Logistics

If you have more than one playground near your home, visit them all and evaluate which one seems to have a friendlier atmosphere or children closer to the ages of your children. It might seem silly, but there are differences in the atmosphere of playgrounds.

- Come prepared! In addition to the usual supplies (see "On the Go with Children" section), bring the following:
- Snacks or lunch—pretzels, cut up fruit or vegetables, yogurt, crackers, sandwich, cheese, crackers, juice, popcorn, small bagels with butter or cream cheese, raisins, and something to drink. Bring extra napkins. Buy your child a plastic lunchbox with Thermos to keep the snack/lunch in. Your child will delight in opening and closing the lunchbox by herself.
- Band-Aids—always come in handy for the little scrapes. Band-Aids with pictures sometimes work miracles on playground "hurts."
- Wet paper towel or washcloth in a plastic bag for cleaning dirty hands and faces.
- Sand and water toys, riding toys, balls, bubbles to blow, and so on. Write your name on every toy. It's more than likely that another child will bring the exact same playthings to the playground. Don't take out all the toys at once. I lost many toys when I would take them all out in one area of the playground, and before I knew it my kids would be off to a different part of the park. I would lose track of what I brought, and it would become a major project to round up all of our belongings.

For the Working Parent

Just as parents socialize, so do baby-sitters and housekeepers. Arrange for your sitter to take your child to the playground on a regular basis, and ask which children your child continually seems to play with at the playground. Get names and phone numbers to contact the parents and arrange to meet at the playground on the weekend.

Play Dates

Invite another child to your home or arrange to visit another child for a limited period of time, perhaps 1½ to 2 hours. At this age, the parent or baby-sitter usually stays while the children play. Never arrange a date around your child's normal nap time. If your child has a special toy or a favorite stuffed animal, put it away so there won't be a major battle if the visiting child wants to play with it. Sharing is very hard for children at this age. One of my children was fine when he went visiting, but when he had friends over, he wouldn't share. In order to put a stop to the continuous tears, I arranged to meet with other parents and children at neutral space, such as the museum, the park, the playground, or at McDonald's.

Toddler Activity Groups

These activities, lasting from 1 to 2 hours, include swimming, music, dance, movement, gym, storytelling, and arts and crafts. A parent or baby-sitter is usually required to attend with the child and participate in the activity. Groups focus on enjoyment of the activity rather than acquisition of skills. The classes are sponsored by a variety of organizations such as local Y's, community centers, art schools, music schools, dance schools, and religious organizations. Fees vary depending on whether the sponsor is nonprofit or profit. (See suggestions for locating activities on pages 185–87.)

Toddler Centers

Similar to part-time nursery schools, toddler programs are run by an educational staff and housed in some licensed facility, such as a church or synagogue, a Y or a school. Children attend two to three mornings or afternoons a week. This type of program allows the child to work with new materials and equipment in a small group setting, enabling him to develop socialization skills such as listening, sharing, and waiting turns. Some children are ready for this experience, whereas others need more time at home in a one-to-one relationship.

If you decide on a toddler program for your child, try to select a center that has a full-time nursery school which your child can eventually attend, for an easy transition. Use the same criteria outlined in the "Selecting a Nursery School" section.

Play Groups

Usually organized by mothers who know each other and want their children to participate in an informal play situation, the group usually has four to six members. Most play groups meet at a different member's home each week with the host-parent and child responsible for planning activities and providing a snack for that meeting. Often, another parent or a hired assistant helps out.

Have an initial planning meeting to decide on your group's goals and the responsibilities of each member. Concentrate on the following areas:

- Will there be a basic plan that every meeting will follow, or will the hosts be free to decide on a format?
- Can a host mother with younger children at home run the group and care for her other kids at the same time?
- If a child doesn't want his mother to leave, should she stay for the meeting?
- Snacks! Make sure you all agree on the nutritional value of the food served. If your group meets at midday, also discuss the kind of lunch foods you find acceptable.

Planning Your Play Group Day

Plan your day! The following is a schedule I used in my play group with Marc. The group met from 10:00 A.M. to 11:45 A.M. The schedule was as follows:

10:00–10:30 Children arrived & free play
10:30–11:00 Organized activity
11:00–11:15 Snack
11:15–11:30 Organized activity
11:30–11:45 Organized activity

Arranging Activities

The organized activities might be:

Arts and crafts (see pages 152–57)
Music and singing (see pages 179–84)
Movement and exercise
Story time (see pages 164–76)
Science projects
Joint building block project
Cooking.

Be flexible! If any activity is not holding the children's attention, be ready to move into another. Always have a few extras planned. As a general rule, alternate a quiet activity with a noise activity.

Set up all the materials and equipment ahead of time. It only takes 5 minutes to lose control of the group while you are looking for the book or setting up the record player or cutting up the apples for snacks.

There are a variety of projects to do with your play group. Consult the following book for suggestions:

The Playgroup Handbook by Laura Peabody and Nancy Towner Butterworth (St. Martin, 1974).

Nursery School

Nursery school is often a child's first step toward independence without the support and watchful eye of parents or baby-sitter. Children in nursery school learn to play, share, and disagree with other children in an ongoing group situation. New materials, equipment, and activities are introduced to help stimulate intellectual, emotional, and physical development.

As our children become involved with school, so do we. The school becomes a neighborhood anchor, supporting parents in the challenges of parenthood. In addition, my children and I formed many close friendships that have continued throughout the years. Nursery school should be a place where both you and your child feel comfortable. Let this be your guiding rule in selecting a school.

Most nursery schools are privately funded with money coming primarily from tuition. However, there are some schools that offer scholarships, sliding scale tuition, or low tuition as a result of a sponsoring agency or organization offsetting some of the cost (such as a religious organization). In some areas the federal government provides free early childhood education programs for families that meet certain economic criteria. The best known is Head Start.

For those of you faced with numerous options, the following guidelines will help you narrow down the choices in some orderly way.

Selecting a Nursery School

You should plan to apply in the fall of the year preceding the year your child will attend.

1. Think about what you consider important in a nursery school.
    *   Philosophy. Is the emphasis on socialization or skills?
    *   Distance. Will you be able to walk or drive? Is there private bus service or will you take public transportation?
    *   Location. If it is a neighborhood school, your child's friends will live nearby.
    *   Religious affiliation.
    *   Parent involvement. This could range from an occasional meeting, conference, social or fund-raising event to a full-scale parent cooperative where parents make school policy and hire the teachers.
    *   Size of program.
    *   Heterogeneous mix. Do you want an economic, ethnic, and racial balance?
    *   Cost of the program.
    *   Scholarships.
    *   Long-range view. Does the school offer programming options? You might want a part-time schedule for your child the first year, but longer hours the second year. Or you might prefer a school that will offer a continuing summer program and a full-day kindergarten as well. Your life will be so much easier if you don't have to look for alternative programs to fill the gaps for the next couple of years.

2. Obtain a list of nursery schools in your community. To obtain a list:
    *   Speak to other mothers.
    *   Each state or large city delegates an agency to license and oversee early childhood nursery schools. Write or call the office of the following and ask for the name, address, and telephone number of the agency that licenses and supervises nursery schools in your community.
        *   The mayor
        *   Your local congressional representative
        *   Your state senator
    Once you have the name of the agency, write or call and ask for a list of nursery schools in your geographic area. Ask for a list of private as well as government funded programs.

3. Call the schools on your list whose descriptions fit your needs, and check out the following:
    *   Admission procedures
    *   Information on the school and an admission form.
    *   Permission to visit the school before or after you apply.
    *   Information on the child's visit to the school. Some schools have

a first-come first-served admission policy and don't interview the child, whereas others screen all applicants.

4. Once you receive the materials from the various nursery schools, narrow your selection to a few and then visit a few programs as a basis of comparison. (Don't visit too many, or you will only get confused.) Then, send in your application form to a select few.

Visiting Nursery Schools

Each school has its own policy for visiting and observing the classroom. It can be quite disruptive to children if there is a constant stream of visitors to the room. However, the school should allow at least ½ hour for prospective parents to meet with the director and comparable time to observe the classroom.

Questions to Ask the Director

Administrative:

- Is the program licensed? By which agency?
- If the program is not licensed, why not?
- Although each state varies in requirements for licensing early childhood programs, a licensed school will at least meet basic standards for health and safety.
- Is the nursery school affiliated with a larger institution (Y, religious organization, community center, a university, etc.)? What is the relationship?
- How long has the school been in operation?
- Up-to-date immunizations and a medical examination should be mandatory for each child.

Staff:

- What are the qualifications of the director, the teachers, and other staff in the classroom? How many teachers have a master's degree in early childhood education?
- How many children in a class?
- What is the ratio of staff to child in the classroom?
- The federal interagency requirements for day-care staff–child ratio is as follows:
  For children 3 to 4 years of age—1 teacher to 5 children
  For children 4 to 6 years of age—1 teacher to 7 children

- What is the supervision and ongoing training of the classroom teaching staff?

Parent:

- What is the role of parents at the school?
- What lines of communication are developed between teacher and parent?
- What is the philosophy of the school? Does it emphasize skill development or socialization? How is this reflected in programming?
- What are the strengths and weaknesses of the program?
- Are there any plans to improve the weak areas?
- Is there a balance between active and quiet activities? Between free-time and scheduled activities?
- Are there any special programs for gym or music?
- Are they taught by specialty teachers?
- How often do the children play outdoors?
- Is there an outdoor play area or nearby park?
- How is a child's adjustment to the program handled?
- How do they deal with a child who has a hard time separating from the parent?

The Final Decision

Once you have visited the schools (see pages 137–38, "Evaluate by Observing") you must begin to put all the information together and make a decision. (In some instances, the school will notify you if your child has been accepted.) No school will meet all your requirements, so you will have to compromise. Perhaps it will help in your decision to rate each factor on a scale of importance from 1 to 5. The following is a suggested list of guidelines.

- Emphasis on socialization
- Emphasis on skills
- Small program (one class per age group)
- Large program
- Program options for future years (full day, extended day, kindergarten, summer program)
- Outdoor facilities
- Special activities (gym, music, swimming)
- Good supply of equipment and supplies in the classroom
- Convenient, neighborhood program
- Your child has a friend who will attend the program
- Warm and supportive atmosphere

- Clean
- Spacious rooms
- Equal mix of working and nonworking parents
- Parent involvement
- Staff/child ratio
- Professional director
- Head teachers have master's degree in Early Childhood Education
- Scholarship program
- Cost of the program
- Religious affiliation
- Heterogeneous group (economic, ethnic, and racial mix)

What are your priorities? How do the schools that you visited measure up against your list? The bottom line is whether you feel comfortable with the staff and the philosophy of the program. *Trust your instincts!*

Day Camp

Day camp can be a wonderful experience. In the right camp, a child feels comfortable and self-confident enough to participate in a wide range of activities; he can develop new skills in sports, learn to swim, explore nature, participate in dramatics, arts and crafts, and possibly boating and horseback riding, and develop a sense of independence as well.

The Right Camp for Your Child

To get the best fit between your child and a camp, start by asking yourself some questions about what makes your child comfortable.

- Does your child need support and encouragement when learning a new skill?
- Does he enjoy sports? Is he a good athlete?
- Does he enjoy playing but is not a good athlete?
- Does your child need help in new social situations?
- Is your child friendly and outgoing?
- Is your child timid and shy in a large group?
- How does your child deal with winning and losing?
- Would he enjoy a wide range of activities or a limited selection?

(Some children thrive on many new activities, whereas other children need to focus on fewer activities on a more higher basis.)
- Does he like a varied schedule or one that's the same each day?
- Are there specific activities your child would like to concentrate on?

Explore Your Options

- Ask friends whose children have attended camp. Check your neighborhood for possible local camps. Speak to the parents of your children's friends. (It's great when children can go to camp with friends from school or the neighborhood.) How long have their children attended the camp? Have they visited during the camp season? What are the strengths and weaknesses of the camp?
- Look in the Yellow Pages of your telephone directory.
- Contact The American Camping Association. This organization was established over 70 years ago to set camp standards. Their accreditation is based on an evaluation of four basic areas: administration (supervision, health, and safety regulations), personnel (staff to camper ratio based on age of group), the facilities, and the program. The Association publishes a directory of over 2,000 accredited day camps, sleep-away camps, and travel camps. The camps are reviewed every three years. There is a fee for this directory. The Association also provides fee counseling service for parents, to help in the selection of a camp. Call or write the national headquarters to locate the regional office near you.

  National Camping Association
  Bradford Woods
  Martinsville, Indiana 46151
  (317) 342-8456
- Decide your price range. Some day camps can be as expensive as sleep-away camps.

How to Evaluate a Day Camp

I have learned from experience that it helps to visit the camp yourself and speak to parents whose children have attended the camp. *If at all possible, visit the camp the summer before you apply.* By seeing the camp in action, you will be able to assess the program in operation. You will get a feeling for the type of staff the director hires, how the day is organized, and whether the children seem happy.

Here are some guidelines for evaluating two common types of day-camp programs: nursery camp and the full-day day camp:

Nursery Camp

The nursery camp is usually an outgrowth of a school program or included as a special program in a day camp.

It is important that a day-camp program be low-keyed for the 2- to 6-year-old group. Groups should be small. Continuity of children and staff is important: Children should be scheduled for not less than 4-week periods; the same staff should work for the entire season. The program should have its own outdoor play area where the children can spend a majority of their day (look for shade!). The indoor facilities should have a good selection of materials, equipment, and pets geared for preschoolers (blocks, dollhouse, dress-up area, puzzles, puppets, arts and crafts, books, records, sand and water play table). Check to see that there is a large space for setting up an indoor playground for very hot or rainy days.

- How many children from the winter nursery program attend the summer program? Do they try to keep the group together? How do they integrate a new child into the program? Will they honor a request to place your child with children he knows?
- How many children are in a group?
- What is the ratio of staff/children? How many counselors are professional teachers and how many are high school or college students?
- Explore the program. What is a daily schedule like? How are the facilities? Are trips planned?
- Do the children go swimming? Or is there a wading pool or sprinkler?
- How many groups attend an activity at the same time?
- Is transportation provided?
- Is lunch included, or do the children bring sandwiches?
- What is the policy when a child has difficulty adjusting? Can the parent stay in the room? Is there enough staff to help a new child adjust?

Full-Day Camp

Day camp is usually a full-day program for children 5 to 14 years old. The following are some concerns you should have if you are considering this option:

- GENERAL How old is the camp? What is the camp size (75—

150 small; 150–400 medium; 500 and over large). If camp is on the large size, do they have divisions for age groups, supervisors of divisions, or separate facilities? Does camp have medical and accident insurance? What are medical facilities on premises and emergency procedures?

- PROGRAM Balanced activities? Two swims a day? How long is an activity period? What are the indoor facilities and activities for inclement weather? What time do activities begin in morning and end in the afternoon? How is competition handled? (Does the camp have intra- or intercamp games? Do they have Olympics or other kinds of competition?) Do campers have a choice in selecting activities? How are skills taught (group or individual instruction)? Does the program change to meet the needs of older campers? Are there greater options for activities? Is there a sleep-over program for overnight, one week, or weekend trip? This could be a good introduction to sleep-away camp, which many children start when they are about 9 years old.
- GROUPS How many children in a group? What is the ratio of counselors to campers (are counselors in training included)? How many campers in an activity group (although your child may be in a small group, he may have an activity combined with other groups).
- STAFF How long has the director been with the camp? How many staff return? Who heads the water program? He or she must be a water safety instructor! Age of staff, camping experience, and professional or educational background are all important. Does the camp have specialists in waterfront activities, athletics, tennis, arts/crafts, gymnastics, and so on? How long have they been with the camp?
- FACILITIES How many areas does camp have? How much space is used for actual activities and how much is unused land? What are the facilities for swimming, sports, tennis, arts and crafts, nature, gymnastics? What space do they use for inclement weather? Does each camper or group have a place for personal belongings, for relaxing, and for group meetings? Are the facilities large enough to handle the number of campers?
- FOOD Does the camp serve meals and snacks? If not, are there facilities for storing lunches and snacks brought from home?
- COMMUNICATION BETWEEN CAMP AND HOME What system is worked out for sharing concerns or problems between camp and home?
- TRANSPORTATION How long does it *really* take to get to camp? The vehicle should have seat belts. More than 16 children should have additional staff with driver. Who is the driver? Professional

driver or counselor? Is the driver experienced in driving groups of children?

Getting References from the Camp Director

Ask for the names of two parents whom you can call. At least one family should have children close in age to yours. Ask the parents the following:

- Did their children like the camp?
- How did you find out about the camp?
- How many years have their children attended the camp?
- Have they visited the camp? What were their impressions?
- What are the strengths and weaknesses of the camp (program, staff, director, facilities, and equipment)?
- Would they select the camp again and why?
- Have they ever had a complaint or problem? How has the director dealt with it?

Making the Decision

Put all your information together and trust your instincts. You may not find the perfect day camp, but you should be able to find one that meets most of your requirements. Later, when your child is 7 years and older, he should be involved in the process of selecting his own camp. Let him visit and speak to the director. You can then evaluate the information and come up with a selection together.

Birthday Parties

We all have different ideas about birthday parties for our children. Some of us prefer traditional parties in our own homes with homemade cakes and goodies and favorite games. Others like the convenience of birthday parties held at a local family restaurant or, with older children, at a skating rink, the movies, the circus, or some other recreation center. The type of party that you choose will depend on your child's age, budget or space restraints, the time factor, and the number of children invited.

Every year I promised myself that the next party would run more smoothly, but each year I found I'd forgotten some vital fact. When my children were very young, for instance, I didn't plan enough activities and the parties ran too long. On Erik's seventh birthday, he wanted to go ice-skating, and I didn't think I had to plan much at all. Before the fun could really begin, though, my husband and I realized that we needed at least two more pairs of hands to lace up the skates of 12 impatient little guests!

Here are some suggestions to make your kids' birthday parties as much fun for *you* as for them.

Birthday Goodies

Although cake and ice cream are traditional fare for birthday parties, you have several options for the desserts. Try cupcakes, ice cream cake, brownies, or large cookies with icing.

Kids will enjoy birthday goodies whether they are store-bought or homemade, but if you would like to make your own, try the Vegetable/Fruit breads recipes on pages 16–17, or the following recipes for brownies or cookies. All are made with *no milk* for the allergic child!

AUNT HAZEL'S BROWNIES

---

2 cups sugar
4 eggs
1 tsp vanilla
1 cup all-purpose flour
2 sticks of butter or margarine

4 squares unsweetened
   chocolate

1. Preheat oven to moderate (350°). Grease 13 × 11 inch × 2 inch baking pan.
2. Mix sugar, eggs, and vanilla. Add the flour until well blended.
3. Melt the chocolate and butter in a double boiler. Add immediately to batter.
4. Pour batter in pan and bake for ½ hour. Check with toothpick. If not quite ready, bake for another 5 to 10 minutes.

When brownies are completely cooled, remove from pan. Frost and decorate.

EMILY'S BIRTHDAY COOKIES

This recipe is great for the home birthday treat or for school birthday celebrations. Just bake, frost and decorate. You might have the children decorate their own cookies by having a set of special decorations for each child (small cup of icing with ice-cream stick, cup of raisins, shredded coconut, chocolate chips, miniature marshmallows, etc.).

Make one design for the birthday cookies. It prevents problems of sharing at the party. Choose either the gingerbread boy, hearts, or circles. The cookie cutters should be 4 inches, which enables the child to have a large enough cookie to decorate.

2 cups butter	2 tablespoons baking powder
2 cups sugar	8–9 cups all-purpose flour
6 eggs	1 egg beaten with 1 tablespoon
1 tsp vanilla	of water added

1. Preheat oven to 375°.
2. Cream the butter then gradually beat in sugar.
3. Beat eggs then add to butter-sugar mixture until well blended.
4. Stir in vanilla.
5. Mix flour and baking powder.
6. Add flour mixture slowly to butter mixture until all is blended in.
8. After the dough is cut into shapes, brush cookies with egg/water mixture.
9. Bake for approximately 30 minutes or until golden brown around the edges.

Energy Savers for Home Birthday Parties

- Allow only 1½ to 2 hours for the party. Timing is important. If you allow 15 minutes for the children to arrive, 8 to 15 minutes to sing "Happy Birthday" and eat the cake, the remainder of the time you must plan for.
- Put away any special toys, games, or dolls that your child doesn't want to share, as well as expensive toys that can break.
- Place a plastic cloth under the table to catch spills and crumbs. (Place the cloth on the floor with a birthday tablecloth over it if the children will be eating picnic style.)
- Have party bags filled with a few inexpensive party favors. Write name of each child on the individual bags. The favors can be handed out to announce that the party is over. Many times it

helps children leave the party if they know the bag is waiting at the door for them to take home.

- Use a bicycle pump to blow up balloons.
- Be sure to have a camera on hand. A nice idea for thank you notes: a picture postcard made from photos taken at the party.
- Offer only one flavor of ice cream and one kind of beverage or you will go crazy trying to take individual orders. If you have time or space in advance, prepare balls of ice cream and freeze and pour drinks and refrigerate.
- Think about the activity you have selected. Do you have enough adults to help and supervise? If not, ask some parents to stay or hire a teenager. Remember, any activity or game that eliminates children is a potential source of spoiled fun and tears. Plan some activity for the children who have been eliminated, to avoid any problems.

Hints for Parties Outside Your Home

If you have limited space or prefer to have your child's party outside your home, you have several options:

- Try your local religious organization or community centers to rent space for the party.
- Hire a commercial party planner.
- Hold the party at a local family restaurant or ice-cream store.
- Older children will enjoy party activities such as bowling, skating, movies, swimming, gymnastics, kite-flying, sleep-overs, sports events, and magic shows.

Parties for 1- to-3-Year-Olds

For this age group, it is important to keep the party simple. Have a limited number of children. The party should be between 1 to 1½ hours long. Inform parents that they are expected to stay. Cake and playing are just fine. A simple craft project or easy game is also a good idea. Do not hire a clown, puppeteer, or any other professional entertainer. The children are too young and may be frightened by this type of entertainment. If you need someone to help out, try hiring your veteran baby-sitter or call a local nursery school for a list of their teaching assistants.

- Because very young children have trouble sitting on a chair at the table, have the children sit around a party tablecloth on the floor. Use only spoons. Little ones may have difficulty using a fork.

- If possible, do not open the birthday presents during the party. Many children have a hard time understanding that the present they bring for the party is not theirs.

Parties for 4- to 6-Year Olds

Children of this age need some form of organized activity, such as arts and crafts projects, games, cartoons, films (see if you can rent one from your local library), clowns, puppet shows, magicians, mimes, guitar sing-a-long, or storyteller, and so on. Check out your local museum for some birthday party programs.

Parties for 7 Years and Up

For this age group, try party activities such as bowling, skating, movies, swimming, gymnastics, kite flying, sleep-overs, sports, and magic shows. At this stage, it's safe to open and admire the gifts.

Gifts

Although I have two children, I still needed suggestions on what to buy my cousin's newborn baby. The same was true when buying birthday gifts for my children's friends. I was also unprepared when relatives or friends asked me what my kids like for birthdays or holidays.

I hope these gift ideas will offer some guidance. In addition to this section, also check out the listings of books, magazines, toys, clothing, games, arts and crafts, and sporting goods in the previous chapters. When the gift is right, gift-giving is a real joy.

Be creative with the wrapping! Children love the wrapping almost as much as the gift. Sometimes I tape lollipops or bubble gum to the wrapping paper; if the gift is the right size, I put it in a small decorative bag, and tie with a bow. Use your imagination and give your wrappings some style.

Gifts for the Newborn

This might seem an unnecessary area to explore, but just imagine having a new baby and 20 gifts to return! The following are some guidelines.

When people ask what you need, don't be shy. Give them three ideas and specify the store. If gifts are bought nearby, return or exchange is simple. It is much easier to return 20 gifts at one store then 10 gifts at 10 different stores. Recommend stores where you have a charge account or stores that pick up. Tell people if they are going to buy clothing, to buy size six months and up. Babies grow fast and will not get good wear out of any clothing that is any smaller.

Let's say that your baby is born in June; a heavy sweater, sweatshirt, snowsuit, hat and scarf, corduroy overalls in size 12 months will be ideal for the baby during the winter months.

- *Reasonable—up to $10* bib, booties, rattles, bank, fancy fitted crib sheets, stuffed animals, clothing (size 6 months or larger), wall hangings, toys for crib or carriage, music box, stretch suit, ball, book or record, baby book/picture album, fancy cobbler's apron for Mom
- *Moderate—$10 to $25* feeding dish, comb and brush set, clothing, toys, picture album with film, baby food grinder, changing pad, quilt or blanket, picture frame, free baby-sitting service, clothing decorated with name of child, stuffed animals, musical mobile for crib
- *Expensive—$25 and up* infant seat, rocking horse, snowsuit, carriage blanket, picture frame, car seat, high chair, playpen, stroller, clothing, swing, baby carrier, bounce chair, diaper service, free baby-sitting service, toys, photographs of baby by child photographer, Polaroid camera
- *6 months to 12 months* Mobiles (choose those with sound and movement), rattles, clutch balls, squeaky rubber toys, bath toys, small stuffed animals, musical balls, music boxes with motion, and books.
- *12 months to 2 years* Stuffed animals, soft dolls, pull toys, large balls, bath toys, pounding benches, nesting toys, first telephone, puzzles with 4 to 5 pieces, rocking horse, trucks, riding toys, records (especially those by Tom Glazer, Pete Seeger, and Ella Jenkins), and books.
- *2 years to 3 years* Plain wooden blocks, shape sorting boxes, cars and trucks, large Lego, large beads, puzzles with 5 to 7 pieces, dolls, water and sand toys, Play-Doh, poster paints, construction

paper, Magic Markers, crayons, pegs and pegboard, musical instruments, books. Large wheeled toys. Clothing with fad characters.

• *3 years to 5 years* Blocks, wooden train sets, transportation toys, neighborhood worker play figures, stringing beads, puzzles with 8 to 15 pieces, Lego sets, rhythm band sets, bikes, balls, tunnel of fun, simple games (Winnie the Pooh, Candy Land, Lotto, Chutes & Ladders), art equipment (paint, crayons, tape, small scissors). Large magnet, magnifying glass, medical kit, learning clock, puppet socks, books, tape recorder, tapes, dolls, and accessories.

• *5 years to 7 years* Blocks, reading and number games, woodworking set with real tools, dominoes, puzzles, checkers, board games, dolls and carriage, dollhouse, two-wheeler bicycle with training wheels, simple microscope, ant farm, walkie-talkie, clay, paints, harmonica. Books, record player, and records. The latest fad in action or theme figures and accessories such as Star Wars, G.I. Joe, Annie, Strawberry Shortcake, Smurfs, Transformers, Robots.

• *7 years and up* At this point the child's interest will be your best guide. Some possibilities are: science projects, advanced Lego, board games, computer learning games, gymnastic equipment, sports equipment, ice and roller skates, two-wheeler bicycle, and books. Dollhouse furniture and accessories, dolls, makeup, jewelry, purses, arts and crafts, sports clothing and accessories, magazines, records, and tapes.

Suggestions for Gifts $5 and Under

Bank, puzzles, coloring books that are informational, color-me posters with pens, Matchbox cars, books, paper, small plant, seeds/dirt/flower pot, fancy socks, fancy jars for storage (nonbreakable), stamp book, playing cards (Old Maid/Go Fish), checkers, belts, umbrella, pom-pom for skates, Christmas ornaments, stamp and pad, kites, action figure people, watercolor paint set, lunch box, diary, stationery and pen, magnifying glass, kaleidoscope, fan, loom and hook, slipper socks, small flashlight with chain, clay, jump rope, jacks and ball, dominoes, plastic figure sets (farm, army, boat, cars), paint by numbers, bingo, board games, fish and bowl, stickers and sticker book magnet, sewing set and felt. Bubble bath, soap carved in fad character, ball, bubbles, fancy shoelaces, a whistle, barrettes, ribbons, balloons with name imprinted, marbles, finger puppets, buttons, small note pad and pencil, small plant.

P.S. Kids can always use new crayons or Magic Markers and paper.

Memories

My sons are always asking me to tell stories about them. Even though I received the Baby Diary Books, I never had the time to fill in all the details. So I'm glad I jotted down facts and some fond memories. Just by making a few notes, you can share your memories with your children when they are old enough to appreciate them. The chart I've prepared is a good guide to keeping track of those memories.

Birth

- Date and day of week_____
- Time_____
- Place_____
- Height and weight_____
- Eye and hair color_____
- Obstetrician_____
- Pediatrician_____

Memorable Firsts

- Home address_____
_____
- Room_____
_____
- Smile_____
- Rolled over_____
- Sat up_____

- Laugh_____
- Tooth_____
- Crawl_____
- Drank from a cup_____
- Steps_____
- Words_____
- Sentence_____
- School_____
- Teacher_____

Special Occasions

- Birthday parties_____
  _____
  _____
  _____
  _____

- Holidays_____
  _____
  _____
  _____
  _____

Favorite Things

- Foods_____
  _____
- Toys_____
  _____
- Stories_____
  _____
- Songs_____
  _____
- Activities_____
  _____
- Adventures_____
  _____

Resources for Parents

The following national organizations will provide you with valuable information as well as help you locate a chapter near your home.

The American Red Cross
National Headquarters
430 17th Street, N.W.
Washington, D.C. 20006
(202) 737-8300

Focus: Classes and publications on parenting and first aid.

The American Society for Psychoprophylaxis in Obstetrics (Lamaze)
1840 Wilson Boulevard
Suite 204
Arlington, Va 22201
(703) 524-7802

Focus: Classes and literature on the Lamaze method of natural childbirth. They also have exercise programs and parenting workshops.

National Organization of Mothers of Twins Club, Inc.
5402 Amberwood Lane
Rockville, Maryland 20853
(301) 460-9108

Focus: Information and referral network to local support groups.

YMCA of the USA
101 North Wacker
Chicago, Ill 60606
(800) USA-YMCA

Focus: National organization for local Young Men Christian Associations. Can provide information on local parenting, toddlers and child center programs.

*International Childbirth
Education Association*
P.O. Box 20048
Minneapolis, Minn 55420
(612) 854-8660

Focus: Book Center with free
catalog on childbirth education.
Can provide information & local
resources on childbirth and
parenting.

J.W.B. (Jewish Welfare Board)
Program Development
15 East 26th Street
New York, N.Y. 10010
(212) 532-4949

Focus: National organization for
all the Jewish Community
Centers and YM-YWHA'S in the
country. Can provide
information on local parenting,
toddlers and child center
programs.

La Leche League
9616 Minneapolis Avenue
P.O. Box 1209
Franklin Park, Ill 60131-8209
(312) 455-7730

Focus: Literature and classes on
breastfeeding, childbirth and
parenting.

National Board of YWCA
Program Division
726 Broadway
New York, N.Y. 10003
(212) 614-2700

Focus: National organization for
local Young Women Christian
Associations. Can provide
information on local parenting,
toddlers and child center
programs.

---

*United States Consumer Product
Safety Commission*
Bureau of Information &
Education
Washington, D.C.
(800) 638-2772

Focus: A 24-hour, toll-free
information center on product
safety. They also provide written
Guides on various areas on
product safety.

Your Household Employee and Social Security

The following information is from the official publication of the U.S. Department of Health and Human Services, Social Security Administration, SSA Publication No. 05–10021, January 1982, U.S. Department of the Treasury, Internal Revenue Services. If you want more information about Social Security monthly benefits, Medicare, or SSI, contact any Social Security office. To find the address of the nearest office, look in the phone directory under "Social Security Administration," or ask at your post office.

Note: If you don't file and pay Social Security taxes, you won't be eligible for federal and state child-care tax credits. The IRS gives penalties for failure of the employer to file.

Reporting Wages

If you pay a household worker $50 or more in cash wages during a three-month calendar quarter, you must deduct Social Security taxes and report the wages. This includes any cash you pay to cover the cost of bus fare, meals, or a room. Failure to report the wages on time may mean you will have to pay a penalty in addition to overdue taxes.

A calendar quarter is a three-month period that ends on March 31, June 30, September 30, or December 31. If wages average as little as $4 a week, they would add up to at least $50 for the quarter. To report wages, write or call the Internal Revenue Service Center for your state. They will send you the necessary reporting forms as well as information on how to complete them and when to file them.

INTERNAL REVENUE SERVICE CENTER
FOR YOUR STATE

If you live in:	*Mailing Address*
Connecticut, Maine, Massachusetts, New Hampshire, New York (all counties except: Nassau, Rockland, Suffolk, and Westchester), Rhode Island, Vermont.	Internal Revenue Service Ct Andover, MA 05501
New Jersey, New York City, and counties of Nassau, Rockland, Suffolk, and Westchester	Internal Revenue Service Ct Holtsville, NY 00501
Delaware, District of Columbia, Maryland, Pennsylvania, Puerto Rico, Virgin Islands, outside United States	Internal Revenue Service Ct Philadelphia, PA 19255
Alabama, Florida, Georgia, Mississippi, South Carolina	Internal Revenue Service Ct Atlanta, GA 31101
Indiana, Kentucky, North Carolina, Tennessee, Virginia, West Virginia	Internal Revenue Service Ct Memphis, TN 37501
Michigan, Ohio	Internal Revenue Service Ct Cincinnati, OH 45999
Illinois, Iowa, Missouri, Wisconsin	Internal Revenue Service Ct Kansas City, MO 64999
Arkansas, Kansas, Louisiana, New Mexico, Oklahoma, Texas	Internal Revenue Service Ct Austin, TX 73301
Alaska, Arizona, Colorado, Idaho, Minnesota, Montana, Nebraska, Nevada, North Dakota, Oregon, South Dakota, Utah, Washington, Wyoming	Internal Revenue Service Ct Ogden, UT 84201
California, Hawaii	Internal Revenue Service Ct Fresno, CA 93888

Social Security

- Keeping records—For Social Security purposes, all you need are the name, address, and Social Security number of each household worker, and the amount of wages paid. Copy the Social Security number directly from the individual's Social Security card. If an employee does not have a card, he or she should apply for one at any Social Security office.
- Deducting Social Security taxes—You must deduct a percent from your employee's cash wages. Your part of the Social Security tax is an amount equal to this. Check with the IRS for the exact percent.
- Quarterly reports—Within a month after a quarter ends, you must send the taxes and a report of the wages you paid to the Internal Revenue Service. This is done by using IRS Form 942 (Employer's Quarterly Tax Return for Household Employees).
- W-2 after year ends—You also must give your worker IRS Forms W-2 (Wage and Tax Statement) by January 31 after the year in which wages were paid. You generally will receive the forms, together with instructions, from the Internal Revenue Service near the end of the year.

Mail Order

For the working parent, the parent with young children, and for all who enjoy having lots of products to choose from, mail order is a terrific timesaver.

The Beginner Reader's Program
Grolier Enterprises
Sherman Turnpike
Danbury, CT 06816
(203) 597-3500
Ages: 5–8 years
After introductory offer, you receive two books a month. You can return books you don't want.

Carol School Supplies, Inc.
185-04 Union Turnpike
Flushing, NY 11366
(212) 454-0050
Catalog: Free
School supplies, toys, games, arts and crafts, educational material, books, records, etc.

Cerutti Children Enterprises
807 Madison Avenue
New York, NY 10021
(212) RE 7-7540
Catalog: Free
Clothing—Newborn to size 14. Carries French, Italian, and domestic clothes.

Childcraft
Catalog Department
20 Kilmer Road
Edison, NJ 08818
(800) 631-5652
Catalog: Free; ask for catalog "Toys that Teach."
Toys, educational materials, puzzles, records, arts and crafts, dolls and accessories, extensive line of early childhood materials, books, sporting supplies, science and mathematics materials.

Children's Choice
Scholastic Book Service
P.O. Box 984
Education Plaza
Hicksville, NY 11802
(516) 433-3800
Ages: 2–7
After introductory offer, you receive two books every 6 weeks. You can return books you don't want.

213

Terminal Hobby Shop
5619 West Florist Avenue
Milwaukee, WI 53218
(414) 527-0770
Catalog: $3.00–$12.50
Electric trains.

Polk's Model Craft Hobbies, Inc.
Mail Order Department
314 Fifth Avenue
New York, NY 10001
(212) 279-9034
Catalog: $2.00 plus postage.
Preschool toys and games, arts and craft supplies, games, science equipment, models (plastic planes, boats, and military miniatures, trains (Lionel), tools for use of models, radio control equipment of airplanes, boats, cars, and submarines. Plastic car models of all kinds. Paints and accessories for all the above-mentioned model kits.

Sears
EAST
4640 Roosevelt Blvd.
Philadelphia, PA 19132
SOUTH
675 Ponce Del Leon Avenue, N.E.
95 Annex
Atlantic, GA 30395
MIDWEST
925 South Homan Avenue
Chicago, IL 60607
WEST
2650 East Olympic Blvd.
Los Angeles, CA 90051
Catalog: $2.00 (deducted from first purchase)
Everything for children (toys, furniture, equipment, clothing, etc.).

Wicker Garden's Baby
Mail Order
1320 Madison Avenue
New York, NY 10028
(212) 348-1166
Catalog: Free
Traditional cribs, changing tables, and high chairs. Clothing (newborn to 6X), foreign and domestic brands.

Sesame Street Book Club
120 Brighton Road
Clifton, NJ 07012
(201) 778-6948
Ages: 2–7
After introductory offer, you receive two books every month. You can return books you don't want.

The Disney Book Club
Grolier Enterprises
Sherman Turnpike
Danbury, CT 06816
(203) 797-3500
Ages: 2–7
After introductory offer, you receive two books a month. You can return books you don't want.

Eeyore's Books for Children
2252 Broadway
New York, NY 10024
(212) 362-0634
Catalog: $2.00 (includes periodic supplements)
Extensive books, cassettes, and records for children.

Blood's Hammock Grove, Inc.
4549 Linton Blvd.
Del Rey Beach, FL 33444
(305) 498-3400
Catalog: Free
Oranges and grapefruit November 1–May 15.

The Popcorn Factory
Mail Order Department
Lake Bluff, IL 60044
(800) 621-5559 outside Illinois
(800) 972-5858 in Illinois
Catalog: Free
Colorful tins filled with your choice of variety of popcorn, pretzels, nuts, candy, and cookies. Available in 2 gallon to 6½ gallon sizes.

England's Mothercare Catalog
Mothercare Limited
P.O. Box 145
Cherry Tree Road
Watford WD 2 5SH, England
Clothings, toys, accessories, furniture and bedding.

F.A.O. Schwarz
745 Fifth Avenue
New York, NY 10151
(212) 644-9400
Catalog: Free
Extensive selection of toys, dolls and accessories, stuffed animals, games, arts and crafts, electronic games, electric trains, sporting goods, family games, puzzles.

Montgomery Ward & Co.
Catalog Department
Montgomery Ward Plaza
Chicago, IL 60671
(312) 467-2000
Catalog: Free
Everything for children (clothing, toys, books, juvenile furniture and equipment, newborn supplies, and equipment and accessories).

Pearl Paint Co. Inc.
308 Canal Street
New York, NY 10013
(212) 431-7932
Catalog: $1.00
Extensive selection of fine art materials (brushes, canvas, paints, paper, clay, acrylics, and pastels).

J. C. Penney Co.
Catalog Department
1301 Avenue of the Americas
New York, NY 10019
(212) 957-4321
Catalog: $2.00
Everything for children (clothing, toys, books, juvenile furniture and equipment, newborn supplies, and equipment and accessories).

Scandinavian Design Inc.
127 East 59th Street
New York, NY 10022
(212) 755-6078
Catalog: Free
White painted or natural birch wood furniture and furniture systems for children of all ages (newborn and up).

Reading for Parents

To better understand your child's emotional, physical, intellectual, and social development as well as your own growth as a parent, try a few of the following resources:

Magazines

American Baby Magazine
575 Lexington Avenue
New York, NY 10022
(212) 752-0775
Subscription Dept.
For expectant parents and parents with children up to age 3.
You receive 6 *free issues* after which you are able to renew your subscription at a fee. With your initial request for the free 6 issues include your due date.

American Baby Books
American Baby which also publishes a quality line of parenting books which you can get at bookstores or order directly from them.

Mothers Today
Box 243
Franklin Lakes, NJ 07417
(212) 867-4820
Subscription Dept.
For expectant parents through parents with children age 3.
Covers a wide range of topics.

Parents' Magazine
80 New Ridge Road
Bergenfield, NJ 07621
1-(800) 247-5470
1-(800) 532-1272 (for Iowa only)
Subscription Dept.
For expectant parents through parents of adolescents.

Baby Talk
352 Evelyn Street
Paramus, NJ 07652
(201) 679-4400

Subscription Dept.

For expectant parents through parents with children age 3.

Free copies available at obstetricians' and pediatricians' offices and Lamaze instructors. You can also subscribe for a fee and the magazine will be mailed directly to you.

Mothering
Mothering Publications, Inc.
P.O. Box 2208
Albuquerque, NM 87103
(505) 897-3131

Subscription Dept.

For expectant parents through parents with children age 3.

Covers a wide range of topics.

Parent Book Club

Creative Parenting Library
40 Guernsey Street
Box 10209
Stamford, CT 06904

Offers a wide variety of subjects, from pregnancy, birth, and caring for the newborn, to discipline, nutrition, and so on. Book selection is based on the age of the member's child. No minimum purchase and members never have to buy a book unless they want it. They can stop anytime they wish.

Write for further information.

Books

There are hundreds of wonderful books about babies and children and on parenting in general. I have selected only a few favorites to mention here. They are basic books that I've learned to rely on for reassurance and advice.

Breastfeeding

- *The Complete Book of Breast-feeding* by Marvin Eiger and Sally Olds (Bantam, 1976).
- *Preparation For Breastfeeding* by Donna and Rodger Ewy (Doubleday, 1975).

- *The Womanly Art of Breastfeeding* by Le Leche League, International (New American Library, 1983).
- *Nursing Your Baby* by Karen Pryer (Pocket Books, 1977).

The First Year

- *Baby and Child Care* by Dr. Benjamin Spock (Pocket Books, 1984). A wonderful resource book which covers most subjects that a new parent would be interested in.
- *Infants and Mothers: Differences in Development* by T. Berry Brazelton (Delacorte, 1983). Helps parents understand the wide range of developmental differences in babies through following three babies (quiet, average, active) in their first year.
- *The Complete Dr. Salk: An A to Z Guide to Raising Your Child* by Lee Salk (New American Library, 1983).
- *The First Three Years of Life* by Burton L. White (Avon, 1984). Stage by stage developmental approach to understanding your baby's physical, intellectual, and emotional development.

Toddlers and Childhood

Books from The Gesell Institute of Child Development can be quite helpful in understanding your child.

- *Infant and Child in the Culture of Today,* Revised ed., by Arnold Gesell et al. (Harper & Row, 1974).

The First Five Years

- *Your One-Year-Old* by Louise B. Ames (Dell, 1983)
- *Your Two-Year-Old* by Louise B. Ames (Delacorte, 1976).
- *Your Three-Year-Old* by Louise B. Ames (Delacorte, 1976).
- *Your Four-Year-Old* by Louise B. Ames (Delacorte, 1976).
- *Your Five-Year-Old* by Louise B. Ames and Frances L. Ilg (Delacorte, 1979).
- *Your Six-Year-Old* by Louise B. Ames and Frances L. Ilg (Delacorte, 1979).
- *The Child from Five to Ten* revised ed., by Arnold Gesell et al. (Harper & Row, 1977).
- *Youth: The Years from Ten to Sixteen* by Arnold Gesell et al. (Harper & Row, 1956).
- *The Magic Years* by Selma H. Fraiberg (Scribners, 1984). Gives a wonderful understanding of the thought process of children.
- *Toddlers and Parents* by T. Berry Brazelton (Dell, 1976).

Child Rearing
• *Children: The Challenge* by Rudolf Dreikurs and Vicki Soltz (Dutton, 1984).
• *How to Parent* by Fitzhugh Dodson (Signet, 1973).
• *How to Father* by Fitzhugh Dodson (Signet, 1975).

Playing with Your Child
• *Baby Learning Through Baby Play* by Ira J. Gordon (St. Martin, 1970).
• *Child Learning Through Child Play* by Ira J. Gordon et al. (St. Martin, 1972).
• *Playground Handbook* by Laura P. Broad and Nancy T. Butterworth (St. Martin, 1974).
• *How to Play with Your Baby* by Athina Aston (East Wood, 1983).
• *The Mother's Almanac* by Marguerite Kelly and Elia Parsons (Doubleday, 1975).

Health
• *Baby and Child Care* by Benjamin Spock (Pocket Books, 1984).
• *A Sigh of Relief: The Revised Edition of the First-aid Handbook for Childhood Emergencies* by Martin I. Green (Bantam, 1984).
• *The Mothers' and Fathers' Medical Encyclopedia* by Virginia E. Pomeranz, M.D., and Dodi Schultz (Plume, 1984).

Safety
• *Your Children Should Know: Teach Your Children the Strategies That Will Keep Them Safe from Assault and Crime* by Flora Colao and Tamar Hosansky (Bobbs-Merrill, 1983).
• *A Nursery Equipment Buyer's Guide* by the U.S. Consumer Product Safety Commission, Bureau of Information & Education, Washington, D.C. 20207. A free guide.

Cookbooks
• *S.N.A.C.K.S: Speedy, Nutritious, and Cheap Kids' Snacks* by Jan Brink and Melinda Ramm (Plume, 1984).
• *Whole Foods for the Whole Family: La Leche International Cookbook* Edited by Roberta Bishop Johnson (Plume, 1984).
• *Feed Me! I'm Yours* by Vicky Lansky (Meadowbrook, 1974).

Toilet Training
• *No More Diapers* by Joae G. Brooks (Dell, 1982).
• *Successful Toilet Training* by T. Berry Brazelton, Pamphlet No. 751, Service Editor, *Baby Talk Magazine*, 66 E. 34th St., New York, NY 10016.

Index

221